PARENTING
Isn't for
COWARDS

PARENTING
Isn't for
COWARDS

PARENTING ISN'T FOR COWARDS
Copyright © 1987 by James C. Dobson

Unless otherwise indicated, Scripture quotations are from the New International Version of the Bible, published by the Zondervan Corporation, copyright © 1973 by the New York Bible Society. Used by permission. Those marked KJV are from the King James Version.

Study Guide Contributing Writers: Ruth and Jan Willson.

"Leader of the Band" by Dan Fogelberg. © 1981 APRIL MUSIC INC. and HICKORY GROVE MUSIC. All rights controlled and administered by APRIL MUSIC INC. All rights reserved. International copyright secured. Used by permission.

"She's Leaving Home" by John Lennon and Paul McCartney. © 1967 NORTHERN SONGS LIMITED. All rights in the USA, CANADA, MEXICO, and the PHILIPPINES controlled and administered by BLACKWOOD MUSIC INC., under license from ATV Music (MACLEN). All rights reserved. International copyright secured. Used by permission.

ISBN 1-56865-823-0

Printed in the United States of America

This book is affectionately dedicated to the mothers of the world, especially the one to whom I am married, who have dedicated themselves to the care and training of the next generation. They have been maligned, goaded, blamed, and ridiculed in recent years, but most have stood their ground. Quietly and confidently they have continued to love and nourish their children and prepare them for a life of service to God and to mankind. There is no more important assignment on the face of the earth, and I hope this book will make their task a bit less difficult.

JAMES DOBSON

Contents

List of Tables

Chapter One

The Challenge

Have you noticed? Being a good parent seems to have become more difficult in recent years. It never has been all that easy, of course. For one thing, babies come into the world with no instructions and you pretty much have to assemble them on your own. They are also maddeningly complex and there are no guaranteed formulas that work in every instance. The techniques that succeed magnificently with one child can fail bewilderingly with another.

Many parents do not understand this frustrating aspect of child-rearing because they have never experienced it. Through no great achievement of their own, they managed to produce a house full of "easy" children. My wife and I are acquainted with a family like that. They were blessed with three of the most perfect children you are likely to find. All three made straight A's in school, kept their rooms perpetually clean, were musically talented, ate with one hand in their laps, were first-team athletes, spoke politely and correctly to adults, and even had teeth that didn't need straightening! It was almost disgusting to see how well they turned out.

Predictably, our friends awarded themselves complete credit for the successes of their children. They were also inclined, at the drop of a hat, to tell you how to raise yours. Overconfidence oozed from their fingertips.

But then an interesting thing happened. The Lord, who must have a sense of humor, gift-wrapped a little tornado and sent it as a surprise package on the mother's fortieth birthday. That family has been stumbling backward ever since. Their little caboose, who is now six years old, is as tough as nails and twice as sharp. He loves to fight with his parents and already knows considerably more than they. Just ask him. He'll tell you. The funny thing about his parents is that they quit giving childrearing advice shortly after his birth. Their job suddenly got tougher!

When I think of these parents today, I'm reminded of a photograph in my files of an elegantly dressed woman who is holding a cup of coffee. Her little finger is cocked ever so daintily to the side and her face reveals utter self-assurance. Unfortunately, this woman does not yet know that her slip has collapsed around her feet. The caption reads, "Confidence is what you have before you understand the situation." Indeed!

More than one tough-minded youngster has sandblasted the confidence of his parents. That's how he gets his kicks. If you have raised only compliant children who smiled regularly and then hustled off to do your bidding, then beware. You may not yet understand the situation. And the Lord could send *you* a surprise package too. Of this fact I'm certain: If you produce enough babies, you will discover sooner or later that there is nothing simple about human beings . . . of *any* age.

From the mail I receive from parents it is clear to me that many are struggling with their responsibilities at home. To learn why, I asked 1,000 mothers and fathers to describe the frustrations they were experiencing in child-rearing. Their answers were fascinating. Some talked of sticky telephones, wet toilet seats, and knotted shoestrings. Others told the most delightful stories.

I'll never forget the mother who had been cooped up with her toddler for several weeks. In a desperate effort to get out of the house, she decided to take her son to a Muppet movie . . . his first. As soon as they arrived in the theater, the mother discovered a minor technical problem. The child didn't weigh enough to keep the spring seat down. There was nothing left to do but hold this churning, squirming two-year-old on her lap throughout the movie.

It was a mistake. Sometime during the next two hours, they lost control of a large Pepsi and a king-sized box of buttered popcorn! That gooey mixture flowed over the child onto the mother's lap and down her legs. She decided to sit it out since the movie was almost over. What she didn't know, unfortunately, was that she and her son were being systematically cemented together. When the movie was over, they stood up and the mother's wraparound skirt came unraveled. It stuck to the bottom of the toddler and followed him up the aisle! She stood there clutching her slip and thanking the Lord she had taken time to put one on!

Can't you see this mother desperately begging the child to drag her skirt back within reach? Parenthood can certainly be humiliating at times. It also seems specifically designed to irritate us. Tell me why it is that a toddler never throws up in the bathroom? Never! To do so would violate some great unwritten law in the universe. It is even more difficult to understand why he will gag violently at the sight of a perfectly wonderful breakfast of oatmeal, eggs, bacon, and orange juice . . . and then go out and drink the dog's water. I have no idea what makes him do that. I only know that it drives his mother crazy!

Obviously, the parents who participated in our "Frustrations of Parenthood" poll did not just share their humorous experiences. They also provided some surprising and distressing answers. Rather than criticizing their children, as one might have expected, the most common response focused on their own inadequacies as mothers and fathers! Specific answers revealed the great self-doubt so prevalent among parents today:

- "not knowing how to cope with children's problems"
- "not being able to make the kids feel secure and loved"
- "I've lost confidence in my ability to parent."
- "I've failed my children."
- "I'm not the example I should be."
- "seeing my own bad habits and character-traits in my children"
- "inability to relate to my children"
- "dealing with guilt when it seems that I have failed my sons"
- "inability to cope"

- "It's too late to go back and do it right."
- "I'm overwhelmed by the responsibility of it all."

Isn't it incredible to observe just how tentative we have become about this task of raising children? Parenting is hardly a new technology. Since Adam and Eve graced the Garden, 77 billion people have lived on this earth, yet we're still nervous about bringing up the baby. It is a sign of the times.

I'm quite certain that parents in past decades spent less energy worrying about their children. They had other things on their minds. I remember talking to my dad about this subject a few years before his death. Our children were young at the time and I was feeling the heavy responsibility of raising them properly.

I turned to my father and asked, "Do you remember worrying about me when I was a kid? Did you think about all the things that could go wrong as I came through the adolescent years? How did you feel about these pressures associated with being a father?"

Dad was rather embarrassed by the line of questioning. He smiled sheepishly and said, "Honestly, Bo," (his pet name for me) "I never really gave that a thought."

How do we explain his lack of concern? Was it because he didn't love me or because he was an uninvolved parent? No. He prayed for me until the day he died. And as I have said on many occasions, he was a wonderful father to me. Instead, his answer reflected the time in which I grew up. People worried about the depression that was just ending, and the war with Germany, and later the cold war with Russia. They did not invest much effort in hand-wringing over their children . . . at least not until a major problem developed. Trouble was not anticipated.

And why not? Because it was easier to raise kids in that era. I attended high school during the "Happy Days" of the 1950s, and I never saw or even heard of anyone taking an illegal drug. It happened, I suppose, but it was certainly no threat to me. Some of the other students liked to get drunk, but alcohol was not a big deal in my social environment. Others played around with sex, but the girls who did were considered "loose" and were not respected. Virginity was still in style for males *and* females. Occasionally a girl came up pregnant, but she was packed off in a hurry and I never knew where she went. Homosexuals were very weird and unusual people. I heard there were a few around but I didn't know them personally. Most of my friends respected their parents, went to church on Sunday, studied hard enough to get by and lived a fairly clean life. There were exceptions, of course, but this was the norm. It's no wonder my parents were concentrating on other anxieties.

It is also no wonder that parents are more concerned in the present era. Their children are walking through the Valley of the Shadow! Drugs, sex, alcohol, rebellion, and deviant lifestyles are everywhere. Those dangers have never been so evident to me as they are today.

I'm writing this book in the heart of London, where my family has joined me for a couple of months. This wonderful and historic city is also the home of some of the most pitiful young people I've ever seen. Rockers and punkers and druggies are on the streets in search of something. Who knows what? Girls with green and orange hair walk by with strange-looking boyfriends. At least I think they're boys. They wear earrings and have blue "Mohawk" haircuts that stick four inches in the air. While gazing at that sight, a clang! clang! clang! sound is heard from the rear. The Hare Krishnas are coming. They dance by with their shaved heads and monk-like robes. Gays parade arm in arm and prostitutes advertise their services. I stand there thinking, *What in heaven's name have we allowed to happen to our kids?*

The same phenomenon is occurring in the United States and Canada. It is sometimes overwhelming to see what has happened to a value system that served us so well. When my daughter was eighteen, I attended a program put on by the music department at her high school. Sitting in front of me was one of Danae's girlfriends. At intermission we chatted about her plans, and she told me she would soon enroll at the University of California, Berkeley. She had just returned from a visit to the school and mentioned casually that something had bothered her about the dormitory in which she would reside. She had learned that the men and women lived side by side and they also shared the same bathrooms. What concerned this pretty young lady was that there was no curtain on the shower stall!

This is the world in which our children are growing up. Obviously, conservative communities still exist where traditional values are honored. Millions of kids still want to do what is right. But dangerous enticements are there, too, and parents know it. Some live in fear that the dragon of adolescence will consume their sons and daughters before they have even started out in life. That anxiety can take the pleasure out of raising children.

There is, however, another reason for the crisis of confidence that many parents are experiencing today. Mothers, especially, have been placed in an impossible bind. They have been blamed for everything that can conceivably go wrong with children. Even when their love and commitment are incalculable, the experts accuse them of making grievous errors in toilet training, disciplining, feeding, medicating, and educating their youngsters. They are either overpossessive or undernourishing. One psychiatrist even wrote an entire book on the dangers of religious training of all types. Thus, no matter how diligently "Mom" approaches her parenting responsibilities, she seems destined to be accused of twisting and warping her children.

Not only have mothers been blamed by the experts for things beyond their control, but they have also been quite willing to criticize themselves. Consider again the list of statements cited from our poll of parents. Eighty percent of the respondents were women, and their most frequent comment was, "I'm a failure as a mother!" What nonsense! Women have been *taught* to blame themselves in this way and it is time to set the record straight.

I don't believe that the task of procreation was intended to be so burdensome. Of course it is demanding. But parents in the twentieth century have saddled themselves with unnecessary guilt, fear, and self-doubt. That is not the divine plan. Throughout the Scriptures, it is quite clear that the raising of children was viewed as a wonderful blessing from God—a welcome, joyful experience. And today, it remains one of the greatest privileges in living to bring a baby into the world . . . a vulnerable little human being who looks to us for all his needs.

What a wonderful opportunity it is to teach these little ones to love God with all their hearts and to serve their fellowman throughout their lives. There is no higher calling than that!

The book you are reading, then, is intended as a celebration of parenthood. We've had enough of groveling and self-condemnation. What we need now is a double dose of confidence in our ability to raise our children properly. We also need to consider the specific frustrations that prevent us from enjoying our kids while they are young. Toward this end, the chapters that follow will deal with the contest of wills between generations, with the perils of adolescence, with parental burnout and its causes, and with the other stress points that irritate and depress us. There is a more satisfying way to raise children, as I believe the reader will see. And there is no better time than now to apply it. Our sons and daughters will be grown so quickly and these days at home together will be nothing but a distant memory. Let's make the most of every moment.

Chapter Two

The Tough and the Gentle

*I*n the days of the wild and woolly West, a lone cowboy went riding through a valley and came unexpectedly upon an Indian lying motionless on the road. His right ear was pressed to the ground, and he was muttering soberly to himself. "Ummm," he said. "Stagecoach! Three people inside. Two men, one woman. Four horses. Three dapple gray, one black. Stagecoach moving west. Ummmmm." The cowboy was amazed and said, "That's incredible, pardner! You can tell all that just by listening to the ground?" The Indian replied, "Ummmmmm. No! Stagecoach run over me thirty minutes ago!"

When I first heard that story I was reminded of the mothers, bless them all, who are raising one or more rambunctious preschoolers simultaneously. If you are one of them, haven't you had moments like that Indian when you found yourself lying flat on the floor and muttering to yourself, "Mmmmm. Three kids. Dirty hands. Wet diapers. Mud on feet. Tearing through the house. Making me crazy! Help!"?

PARENTING ISN'T FOR COWARDS

If you've been in this posture lately, then take heart. You are not alone. Millions of parents, past and present, can identify with the particular stresses you are experiencing right now. A child between eighteen and thirty-six months of age is a sheer delight, but he can also be utterly maddening. He is inquisitive, short-tempered, demanding, cuddly, innocent, and dangerous at the same time. I find it fascinating to watch him run through his day, seeking opportunities to crush things, flush things, kill things, spill things, fall off things, eat horrible things—and think up ways to rattle his mother. Someone said it best: The Lord made Adam from the dust of the earth, but when the first toddler came along, He added *electricity!*

Adolescents are interesting too, and we'll discuss them at length in later chapters. But toddlers are a breed apart. Bill Cosby said he could conquer the world if he could somehow manage to mobilize about two hundred aggressive two-year-olds. It wouldn't surprise me. His army should definitely include an energetic lad named Frankie who belongs, more or less, to some friends of ours.

Little Frankie is a classic toddler. One day recently he pulled a chair over to the front window and carefully placed it inside the drapes. He was standing there staring out at the world when his mother came looking for him. She spied his little white legs protruding beneath the drapes and quietly slipped in behind him. Then she heard him speaking to himself in very somber terms. He was saying, "I've *got* to get out of here!"

I could fill a book with wonderful pronouncements from the mouths of preschool children. They are among the most delightful little people on the face of the earth.

But returning to our thesis, they (and all children) bring a special kind of stress into the lives of their parents. Humorist Erma Bombeck said in one of her books that she was frustrated by her children from the moment they were born. She remembered *how* she got three kids, but she couldn't recall *why*. She decided maybe they were a 4-H project that got out of hand.

For some parents, the overwhelming responsibility associated with child-rearing is not so funny. As indicated in the preceding chapter, there appears to be a growing number of husbands and wives today who are not coping well with parenthood. They've reached the end of the rope and it is frazzled. The letters they send to me are replete with self-condemnation, guilt, and anger. Many seem to have experienced a kind of physical exhaustion that leaves them confused and depressed.

High on the list of irritants which keeps them off balance and agitated is the tendency of some children to test, challenge, resist, and blatantly defy authority. These rebellious youngsters can create more stress in a single afternoon than their mothers can handle in a week. I wrote about them in an earlier book entitled *The Strong-Willed Child*, but they continue to fascinate me. For fifteen years I have watched them operate and wondered what makes them tick. I have interviewed adults who had been rebellious teenagers, and asked them what they were thinking during their season of anger. Even they do not fully understand themselves. I resolved to investigate further.

On behalf of those readers who have never encountered him, let me describe the tough-minded child. At birth he looks deceptively like his more compliant sibling.

He weighs seven pounds and is totally dependent on those who care for him. Indeed, he would not survive for more than a day or two without their attention. Ineffectual little arms and legs dangle aimlessly in four directions, appearing to be God's afterthoughts. What a picture of vulnerability and innocence he is!

Isn't it amazing, given this beginning, what happens in twenty short months? Junior then weighs twenty-five pounds and he's itching for action. Would you believe this kid who couldn't even hold his own bottle less than two years ago now has the gall to look his two-hundred-pound father straight in the eye and tell him where to get off? What audacity! Obviously, there is something deep within his soul that longs for control. He will work at achieving it for the rest of his life.

In the early 1970s I had the privilege of living near one of these little spitfires. He was thirty-six months old at the time and had already bewildered and overwhelmed his mother. The contest of wills was over. He had won it. His sassy talk was legendary in the neighborhood, not only to his mother but to anyone who got in his way. Then one day my wife saw him ride his tricycle down the driveway and into the street, which panicked his mother. We lived on a curve and the cars came around that bend at high speed. Mom rushed out of the house and caught up with her son as he pedaled down the street. She took hold of his handlebars to redirect him, and he came unglued.

"Get your dirty hands off my tricycle!" he screamed. His eyes were squinted in fury. As Shirley watched in disbelief, this woman did as she was told. The life of her child was in danger, and yet this mother did not have the courage to confront him. He continued to ride down the street and she could only stand and watch.

How could it be that a tiny little boy at three years of age was able to buffalo his thirty-year-old mother in this way? Well, it was clear to any observer that she had no idea how to manage him. But also, he was simply tougher than she—and they both knew it. This mild-mannered woman had produced an iron-willed kid who was giving her fits, and you can be sure that her physical and emotional resources were continually drained by his antics.

Contrast this independent youngster with his easy-going counterpart at the other end of the continuum. The compliant child approaches people from an entirely different direction. He wants to please them because he needs their approval. A word of displeasure or even the slightest frown from his parents can be disturbing to him. He is a lover, not a fighter.

A few years ago I talked with the mother of one of these easygoing kids. She was concerned about the difficulties her son was having in nursery school. He was regularly being bullied by more aggressive children, but it was not within him to defend himself. Thus, every afternoon when his mother came to get him, he had been whacked and harassed by these other boys. Even the girls were joining in the fun.

"You must defend yourself!" his mother said again and again. "Those other children will keep hitting you until you make them stop!"

Each day she urged her little lover to be more assertive, but it contradicted his nature to do so. Finally, his frustration became so great that he began trying to follow his mother's advice. As they were on the way to school one morning he said, "Mom! If those kids pick on me again today . . . I'm . . . I'm . . . I'm going to beat them up! Slightly."

How does one beat up an opponent *slightly?* I don't know, but it made perfect sense to this compliant child. He didn't want to use any more force than was absolutely necessary to survive. Why? Because he had a peaceloving nature. His parents didn't teach it to him. It simply *was.*

As most mothers know, this kind of compliant child and his strong-willed sibling are so distinct that they could almost be from different planets. One cuddles to your embrace and the other kicks you in the navel. One is a natural sweetheart and the other goes through life like hot lava. One follows orders and the other gives them. Quite obviously, they are marching to a different set of drums.

I must make it clear that the compliant child is not necessarily wimpy or spineless. That fact is very important to our understanding of his nature and how he differs from his strong-willed sibling. The distinction between them is *not* a matter of confidence, willingness to take a risk, sparkling personality, or other desirable characteristics. Rather, the issue under consideration is focused on the strength of the will—the inclination of some children to resist authority and determine their own course, as compared with those who are willing to be led. It is my supposition that these temperaments are prepackaged before birth and do not have to be cultivated or encouraged. They will make themselves known soon enough.

Not everyone concurs. Many psychologists and psychiatrists of the past would have disagreed violently with this understanding. Sigmund Freud, the father of psychoanalysis, and J. B. Watson, the creator of behaviorism, believed that newborns come into the world as "blank slates" on which the environment would later write. For them, a baby had no inborn characteristics of personality that distinguished him from other infants. Everything he would become, both good and evil, would result from the experiences to be provided by the world around him. He could make no independent decisions because he had no real freedom of choice . . . no ability to consider his circumstances and act rationally on them. Watson even rejected the existence of a mind, viewing the brain as a simple switchboard that responded automatically to external stimuli. Hence, his system of thinking has been called, "Psychology out of its mind."

Watson bragged during the 1920s that he could train any infant "to become any type of specialist I might select . . . doctor, lawyer, artist, merchant, chief and, yes, even beggarman and thief." He thought children were simply "raw material" for parents "to fashion in ways to suit themselves."

In short, this belief that all behavior is caused is called *determinism*, and it will have significance for us in later discussions. I first heard the concept when I was in graduate school. I didn't accept it then, and I certainly don't believe it now. As a Christian psychologist, I have always filtered man-made theories through the screen of Scripture, and in this instance, determinism hangs up in the wire. If it were true, we would be unable to worship and serve God as a voluntary expression of our love. We would be mere puppets on a string, responding to the stimuli around us.

It is becoming clear today just how far off-base these classical psychologists have been in their interpretation of human behavior. There is no doubt, as they said, that the environment is enormously influential in molding and shaping our personalities, but they failed to recognize our ability to think, to choose, and to respond according to our own temperaments. We are rational human beings who can override our experience and external influences. Furthermore, at birth, except for identical twins, no two of us are alike. And how foolish it was to have thought otherwise. If God makes every grain of sand and every snowflake like no other on earth, how simplistic it was to have believed He mass-produced little human robots. We are, after all, made in *His* image.

A blob of tissue? A blank slate? A mass of protoplasm? Hardly! Individual differences in temperament can be discerned at birth or shortly thereafter. In one remarkable scriptural reference we even see references to a strong-willed temperament before the child was born. Genesis 16:11 reports a striking conversation between an angel of the Lord and Abraham's pregnant servant girl, Hagar. He said, "You are now with child and you will have a son. You shall name him Ishmael, for the Lord has heard of your misery. He will be a wild donkey of a man; his hand will be against everyone and everyone's hand against him, and he will live in hostility toward all his brothers."

Does that sound like anyone you know? I've met a few wild donkeys in my time, to be sure. In another example from the book of Genesis, we are told of the prenatal development of the twins, Jacob and Esau. One was rebellious and tough while the other was something of a mama's boy. They were also enemies before they were born and continued in conflict through much of their lives (see Genesis 25:22–27). Then later, in one of the most mysterious and disturbing chapters in the Bible, the Lord said, "Jacob have I loved and Esau have I hated" (Romans 9:13). Apparently, God discerned a rebellious nature in Esau before he was born and knew that he would not be receptive to the divine Spirit.[1]

Behavioral scientists are now observing and documenting the subtle understandings that have been evident in the Scriptures for thousands of years. One of the most ambitious of these efforts to study the temperaments of babies has been in progress for more than three decades. It is known as the New York Longitudinal Study. The findings from this investigation, led by psychiatrists Stella Chess and Alexander Thomas, are now reported in their excellent book for parents entitled, *Know Your Child.* I recommend it enthusiastically to anyone interested in child development.

To my delight, Chess and Thomas found that babies not only differ significantly from one another at the moment of birth, but those differences tend to be rather persistent throughout childhood. Even more interestingly, they observed three broad categories or patterns of temperaments into which the majority of children can be classified. The first they called "the difficult child," who is characterized by negative reactions to people, intense mood swings, irregular sleep and feeding schedules, frequent periods of crying, and violent tantrums when frustrated.

Does that sound familiar?

The second pattern is called "the easy child," who manifests a positive approach to people, quiet adaptability to new situations, regular sleep and feeding schedules, and a willingness to accept the rules of the game. The authors concluded, "Such a youngster is usually a joy to her parents, pediatrician, and teachers." Amen.

The third category was given the title "Slow-to-warm-up" or "shy." These youngsters respond negatively to new situations and they adapt slowly. However, they are less intense than difficult children and they tend to have regular sleeping and feeding schedules. When they are upset or frustrated, they typically withdraw from the situation and react mildly, rather than exploding with anger and rebellion.

Not every child fits into these categories, of course, but approximately 65 percent do. Chess and Thomas also emphasize that babies are fully human at birth, being able immediately to relate to their parents and begin learning from their environments. I doubt if that news will come as a surprise to most parents, who never believed in the "blank slate" theory, anyway. Ask the mother who has raised a houseful of children. She will tell you that each of her kids had a different personality . . . a different "feel" . . . the first time she held the little one in her arms. She is right.

It should not be difficult to understand why these findings from longitudinal research have been exciting to me. They confirm my own observations, not only about the wonderful complexity of human beings, but also about the categories of temperament identified by Chess and Thomas. Nevertheless, basic questions remain to be answered.

What do we really know about these strong-willed and compliant children? (We'll leave our consideration of the shy child to a future book.) How persistent are their personality traits as they grow older? What are the teen years like for each? How do their parents feel about raising them? Does the strong-willed child have an advantage over the compliant child socially or academically or in achievement during early adulthood? These questions have never been answered, to my knowledge, since we have only recently admitted that temperamental differences exist. It was this dearth of information that led me to initiate a large-scale inquiry of my own into the subject.

Initially, a questionnaire was developed for use with parents (see Appendix). By completing this research instrument, parents provided extensive information regarding their own temperaments and those of their children. Specifically, they were asked to evaluate each mèmber of the family on a five-point scale as follows: (1) very compliant; (2) rather compliant; (3) average; (4) rather strong-willed; (5) very strong-willed. No effort was made to define these categories because my interest was only in those children at the extremes, (categories [1] and [5]). The other records were ignored, except for the provision of demographic information.

I then asked detailed questions about the children and how their parents felt about raising them. More than thirty-five thousand families participated in the study and the data were analyzed at the University of Southern California Computer Center. I was assisted in the analysis by my good friend, Malcolm Williamson, Ph.D., whose specialties are measurement and statistics. We generated a mountain of computerized information that could fill five books this size, but we will just hit the highlights here. Let me say that this has been a fascinating journey into human nature, and I wish to express appreciation to the families who shared their experiences with me. I believe the information I have learned through this effort is available nowhere else in the world.

We'll discuss those findings in the next two chapters.

---

[1] I recognize that this is deep water theologically speaking. Jacob was not rejected by God, and yet he, like Esau, was sinful and disobedient. Who among us can explain God's greater judgment on one than the other? In reference to the analogy between Jacob and Esau and the temperaments of children, I want to make it clear that the strong-willed child is no more evil or ungodly than his compliant sibling. His *inclination* toward disobedience may be greater, but I am certainly not casting them in terms of "good" vs. "bad." They are simply different, and one is more difficult to handle than the other.

Chapter Three

What 35,000 Parents Said about Their Children

*A*ll right, class. I'm ready to distribute your midterm examination. We will soon see how well you understand the differences between very strong-willed and very compliant children. Close your books, please, and clear your desks of everything but pencils. Do not copy from your neighbor. We will discuss the correct answers after you have turned in your completed examination. Any questions? Good. Oh, by the way—if you fail this test you will be required to baby-sit with nine strong-willed toddlers for the next six weeks! You may begin.

Multiple Choice

1. It would be interesting to know when a baby is due whether he is likely to be difficult or easy to raise. Based on our data, we can take an educated guess. What do you think the ratio is between very strong-willed and very compliant children?

    (1)   There are about twice as many very compliant children.

    (2)   There are almost three times as many very strong-willed children.

    (3)   There is about the same number of both.

    (4)   There are about twice as many strong-willed children.

2. Is it tougher to raise boys or girls? The answer may depend in part on the temperaments of each. When we consider only strong-willed children, what is the ratio of males to females?

    (1)   Males outnumber females by about 5 percentage points.

    (2)   Females outnumber males by about 9 percentage points.

    (3)   Males outnumber females by about 31 percentage points.

    (4)   There is no difference between the sexes.

3. Let's consider only easy-to-raise children now. What is the ratio of males to females among these compliant children?

    (1)   Males outnumber females by about 10 percentage points.

    (2)   Females outnumber males by about 6 percentage points.

    (3)   Males outnumber females by about 19 percentage points.

    (4)   There is no difference between the sexes.

4. Select the accurate statement below:

    (1)   Firstborn children are more likely to be very strong-willed.

    (2)   Secondborn children are more likely to be very strong-willed.

(3) Thirdborn children are more likely to be very strong-willed.

(4) There is no strong tendency for temperament to be related to birth order.

5. Select the accurate statement below:
(Answers relate to when the temperament is identified)

(1) Less than 10 percent of very strong-willed children are recognizable at birth to 3 months.

(2) About a third of very strong-willed children are recognizable at birth to 3 months.

(3) The vast majority of very strong-willed children are recognizable at birth to 3 months.

(4) Only a few very strong-willed children are recognizable until toddlerhood, when 98 percent "show up."

6. Is the temperament of the child inherited from the parents?

(1) The data suggest that it is.

(2) The data suggest that it is not.

7. What happens to the rebellious nature of very strong-willed children as they move through the years?

(1) Very few rebel until mid-adolescence, when a peak of 30 percent occurs.

(2) After a peak of 20 percent rebel in toddlerhood, very little rebellion occurs until early adolescence.

(3) Approximately 40 percent rebel in toddlerhood, and the percentages rise in every age category through adolescence, reaching a peak of 74 percent in the teen years.

(4)   Rebellion remains hidden, more or less, until early adolescence when an "explosion" occurs, reaching a peak of 63 percent at fifteen years of age.

8. This next item refers to one of the most important findings from our study. It asks the question, what can be expected from compliant children—those easy, happy, cooperative kids—as they go through adolescence and young adulthood? Do they rebel? If so, how commonly? First, please indicate the percentage of these kids whom you think go into severe rebellion in either adolescence or young adulthood.

(1)   3 percent
(2)   26 percent
(3)   52 percent
(4)   76 percent
(5)   89 percent

9. What percent of very compliant children eventually go into *mild* rebellion in either adolescence or young adulthood?

(1)   14 percent
(2)   33 percent
(3)   41 percent
(4)   79 percent
(5)   91 percent

10. Which individual has an edge in academic achievement during the teen years?

(1)   The very strong-willed child.
(2)   The very compliant child.
(3)   Neither; there is no significant difference between them.

11. Which individual typically makes the best social adjustment in adolescence?
    (1) The very strong-willed child.
    (2) The very compliant child.
    (3) Neither; there is no significant difference between them.

12. One of the characteristics of the compliant child during the early years is the ease with which his parents can mold and shape him. He is very responsive to their leadership. Given that flexibility, how does he respond to peer pressure? Or, asked another way, which child (strong-willed or compliant) is more likely to be "peer dependent" during adolescence?
    (1) The very strong-willed child.
    (2) The very compliant child.
    (3) Neither; there is no significant difference between them.

13. Which individual is more likely to have the higher self-esteem in adolescence?
    (1) The very strong-willed child.
    (2) The very compliant child.
    (3) Neither; there is no significant difference between them.

14. Parents were asked to indicate how their grown sons and daughters had achieved in adult pursuits. Which group do you think succeeded best?
    (1) The very strong-willed.
    (2) The very compliant.
    (3) There was no significant difference between them.

PARENTING ISN'T FOR COWARDS

Well, that's the end of our little quiz. I hope you won't feel too badly if you flunked it. Honestly, I'm not sure I could have passed it before seeing the findings from our study. Apparently, there is broad misunderstanding among parents of these special children with unusually tough or easy attitudes toward authority. Indeed, I administered this quiz to many groups of young parents before writing my book. They didn't do so hot, either. In fact, it was typical for them to get from 4 to 6 items correct. One man answered 12 of the 14 items accurately, and he was given the "Superdad of the Year" award. When asked how he knew so much about very strong-willed and very compliant kids, he replied, "I raised one of each!"

Now, I'll repeat a simplified version of each question from the test, give the correct answer and then provide additional information about the issue at hand.

Question 1: What is the ratio of very strong-willed to very compliant children?
Answer: (4) There are about twice as many very strong-willed children. The entire distribution of 37,372 children was as follows:

Table 1—Ratio of Very Strong-Willed to Very Compliant Children

	Very Compliant	Rather Compliant	Average	Rather Strong-Willed	Very Strong Willed	Totals
Number of Cases	4,340	10,821	9,331	4,981	7,899	37,372
Percentage in Category	11.6%	29.0%	25.0%	13.3%	21.1%	100.0%

28

Actually, the true ratio of very strong-willed to very compliant children is more like 3 to 1 than 2 to 1. Why? Because many of the 4,340 children in the very compliant category, above, were infants who had not yet been recognized as strong-willed. Their parents reported them to be compliant but a surprise is coming their way. When those children under 30 months are eliminated from our analysis, 74 percent of the children being studied were very strong-willed and 24 percent very compliant.

> *Question 2*: What is the ratio of males to females within the category of very strong-willed children?
> *Answer:* (1) Males outnumber females by about 5 percentage points . . . 52.5 to 47.5.

> *Question 3*: What is the ratio of males to females within the category of very compliant children?
> *Answer:* (2) Females outnumber males by about 6 percentage points . . . 53 to 47.

> *Question 4*: Select the accurate statement below (regarding birth order and temperament).
> *Answer:* (4) There is no strong tendency for temperament to be related to birth order.

There is a slight trend toward compliance for firstborn children and strong-willed for secondborn. However, our assumption is that these characteristics are *inborn*, and should not be highly influenced by an environmental factor such as birth order. That is what we found.

Question 5: Select the accurate statement below (regarding the age when the strong-willed child is recognized).
Answer: (2) About a third (36 percent) of very strong-willed children are recognized at birth.

By one year of age, 66 percent are identified and 92 percent by age 3. Compliant children tend to be recognized earlier: 43 percent between birth and three months, 74 percent by one year, and 93 percent by the third birthday.

Question 6: Is the temperament of the child inherited from the parents?
Answer: (1) *Yes.* The data suggest that it is.

Though there are many exceptions, there does seem to be a tendency for the temperaments of the parents to be reproduced in their children. Perhaps the environment has influenced our findings here, but I think genetics played the dominant role. There does seem to be an inherited component, even though it sometimes fails to materialize. It is not uncommon, for example, to produce three or four easy-to-raise children followed by a pistol.

Question 7: What happens to the rebellious nature of very strong-willed children as they move through the years?
Answer: (3) Approximately 40 percent rebel in toddlerhood, and the percentages rise in every age category through adolescence, reaching a peak of 74 percent in the teen years.

The data clearly reveal that the percentage of very strong-willed children who rebel begins high in toddlerhood, (40 percent), and never lets up until adulthood. There is no lull of any significance between toddlerhood and adolescence. This is important information, even though somewhat unpleasant, for parents who want to predict the patterns of behavior from their tough-minded kids. To assist in that understanding, I have plotted the data on the graph below. It depicts the percentage of *strong-willed children only* who rebel at each age category, (upper line), and the percentage who choose to cooperate (lower line). Note that the numbers do not add up to 100 percent because of the uncharted children in the middle who neither rebel nor make a special effort to cooperate.

Table 2—Rebellion and Cooperation in Strong-willed Children

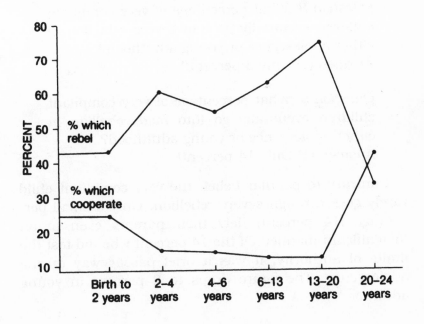

PARENTING ISN'T FOR COWARDS

I hope this information will not be discouraging to parents of strong-willed children. It is true that a significant percentage will be in rebellion at any one time, (from 40 to 74 percent) while the percentage who cooperate ranges from 23 percent to a low of 11 percent in adolescence. It is encouraging, however, to see the rapid decline of rebellion in young adulthood, dropping precipitously from 74 to 36 percent. In fact, the lines cross slightly at that point, with more strong-willed children cooperating than rebelling. The battles are still in progress for about a third of the individuals, but most of the fire is spent. They'll soon join the human race again. I'll share other good news in a moment.

Now we come to a most surprising discovery from the study. It came in answer to questions 8 and 9.

Question 8: What percentage of very compliant children eventually go into severe rebellion in either adolescence or young adulthood?
Answer: (1) Only 3 percent!!

Question 9: What percentage of very compliant children eventually go into *mild* rebellion in either adolescence or young adulthood?
Answer: (1) Only 14 percent!

Contrary to popular belief, the very compliant child rarely goes through severe rebellion. Only a small percentage (14 percent) defy their parents even in an insignificant manner. Of the 14 percent who did test the limits of authority, it was a brief passageway during adolescence. The figure drops to 8 percent in young adulthood.

The findings about *compliant* children are depicted in Table 3, which parallels the one above for strong-willed children. It tells a remarkable story of cooperation and harmony at home.

Table 3—Rebellion and Cooperation in Compliant Children

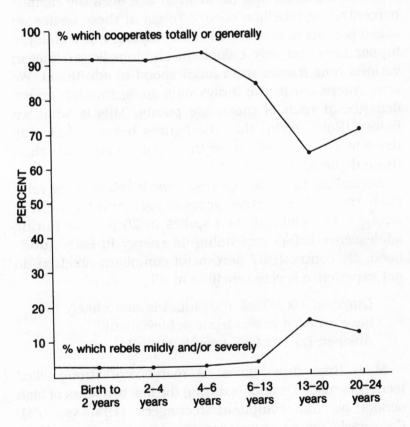

PARENTING ISN'T FOR COWARDS

Isn't it amazing that the vast majority of these compliant children (91 percent) do not become difficult during the terrible twos, and then they remain cooperative up to the time of the adolescent valley? Even during the teen years, only 17 percent go into rebellion (that figure includes mild and severe rebellion).

Finally, we need to look at this same issue from another angle to learn (1) how stable is the tendency to rebel across time, and (2) at what age does the highest percentage of rebellion occur? To get at these issues we asked parents to evaluate their very strong-willed children (upper line) and very compliant children (lower line) in various time frames from toddlerhood to adulthood. We were interested in the individuals going through severe defiance at each of those age points. This is what we found. (Note, again, that the figures below reflect only those in *severe* rebellion, so the numbers are lower than those depicted earlier.)

According to these figures, *severe* rebellion is relatively rare before thirteen years of age, even for the very strong-willed child. It then spikes to 26 percent during adolescence before expending its energy in early adulthood. By contrast, 97 percent of compliant children do not experience severe rebellion at all.

> *Question 10*: Which individual is more likely to have an edge in academic achievement?
> *Answer*: (2) The very compliant child.

More than three times as many very strong-willed teenagers made Ds and Fs during the last two years of high school as did compliant teenagers (19% vs. 5%). Conversely, twice as many compliant adolescents made As

Table 4—Percent of Strong-willed and Compliant Children in *Severe* Rebellion at Various Age Categories

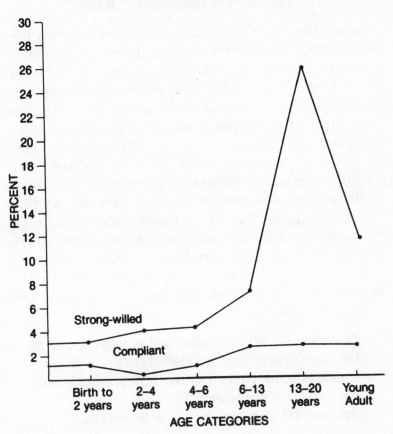

(45% vs. 25%). Of all very compliant teenagers, 79 percent were A and B students, compared with 53 percent of very strong-willed kids. The same pattern was also evident in grades six, nine, and to a lesser degree, in college.

Question 11: Which individual typically makes the best social adjustment in adolescence?
Answer: (2) The very compliant child.

Again, there is a remarkable difference between these two categories of children, favoring the compliant child by a wide margin. During adolescence, 35 percent of the compliant children were said to have "no social problems," compared with only 15 percent of the strong-willed. Likewise, 5 percent of the compliant had "many social problems" compared with 16 percent of the strong-willed. Only 2 percent of the compliant were "generally disliked," but 9 percent of the strong-willed were given this designation. A similar pattern was seen for younger children, as well.

It would appear that the youngster who is challenging the authority of his parents and starting little insurrections at home is also more likely to behave offensively with his peers. We should point out, however, that the majority of strong-willed children do not have great social problems.

Question 12: Which individual is more likely to be "peer dependent" in adolescence . . . that is, which is more easily influenced by group opinion and peer pressure?
Answer: (1) The very strong-willed child.

The compliant teenagers turned out to be considerably less peer dependent than the strong-willed. I had assumed that these kids who had been so easy for their parents to mold and influence would also be more vulnerable to pressure from their peer group. After all, one of their unique characteristics is the desire to please other people. Why wouldn't that sensitivity extend to friends and associates? I even made a statement to that effect in my first film series, "Focus on the Family," during which I stated:

> I am not speaking derogatorily of the strong-willed child. I don't think it's "bad kid vs. good kid." I think the defiant child has greater potential for character development and for accomplishment and leadership. Yes, it is more difficult to raise him.
>
> But maybe the same characteristics that cause a toddler to stamp his foot and say no to you will cause him, thirteen years later, to say no to the peer group when they offer him drugs. We need to shape his will and give him the ability to shape his own impulses.

I was wrong. But no one is perfect. There was an enormous difference in the degree of peer dependency between the two groups of adolescents. Some 58 percent of the strong-willed teenagers were judged by their parents to have been greatly influenced by agemates. This compares with only 24 percent of the compliant adolescents. Since peer dependency is one of the demons behind drug abuse, alcoholism, and sexual promiscuity, this characteristic of strong-willed teenagers is of serious concern to us.

Question 13: Which individual is more likely to have the higher self-esteem in adolescence? *Answer:* (2) The very compliant child.

It is difficult to overestimate the importance of this finding in favor of the compliant child. He is *much* more likely to feel good about himself than his strong-willed sibling. Only 19 percent of the teenagers in this category either disliked themselves (17 percent) or felt extreme self-hatred (2 percent). Of the very strong-willed teenagers, however, 43 percent either disliked themselves (35 percent) or experienced extreme self-hatred (8 percent). The differences were also evident at the positive end of the scale, although they were not quite so dramatic. A picture is emerging of the compliant child being more at peace with himself, as well as being at peace with his parents.

Why do strong-willed children have a greater tendency to doubt their own worth in this way? It is difficult to say, except to affirm that they are more unsettled in every aspect of their lives. We do know that lower self-esteem is related to the excessive peer dependency, academic difficulties, social problems, and even the rebellion we have seen. Acceptance of one's intrinsic worth is the core of the personality. When it collapses, everything else begins to quiver.

> *Question 14*: Finally, parents were asked to indicate how their grown sons and daughters had achieved in their adult pursuits. Which group do you think succeeded best, the strong-willed or the compliant?
>
> *Answer*: (2) The very compliant.

Again, the pattern held . . . 69 percent of compliant children, then as young adults, were considered to be successful or highly successful by their parents. Only 56 percent of the strong-willed were given this accolade. When one looks at the frequency of failure in the same context, the compliant come out winners once more: 11 percent vs. 22 percent.

Most of the parents with whom I have shared these findings have been surprised by the outcome. They expected strong-willed individuals to emerge on top in this category. Their aggressiveness should have produced a faster start, or so the common wisdom goes. On closer examination, however, the compliant young man or woman succeeds in early business pursuits because he plays by the rules. He finds out what the boss wants and promptly gives it to him. It would also appear that he is going through less personal turmoil in this post-adolescent era. He is thereby freer to get on with the business of living.

These findings would not surprise Bill Haughton, a successful real estate broker and former Marine living in Dallas, Texas. He was in the industrial distribution business for thirty years, starting as the first employee and eventually selling the company in 1980 when there were 450 employees in 40 locations. Bill and I have become good friends, and I once asked him how he had selected new employees. His answer was surprising. He said the first thing he wanted to know about any young man who applied for a job was the nature of his relationship with his father. If it was stormy, he would not hire him.

Bill explained his reasoning: "If a boy learned to accept authority under his dad, the chances were good that he would later accept the leadership of his employers. But if he was a rebel, he was more likely to cause difficulties in my business."

I then asked Bill how he screened women. Again, his perspective was unique, even if controversial. He said, "Women are more difficult to assess in the beginning. You don't really know them until they are on the job.

Unfortunately, they can be meaner than men. When I realize I have hired an office malcontent, someone who is always working to get to the head of the pecking order, then I know I have erred. She will create continual morale problems. She must go or my shop will be chaotic!"

Bill Haughton's philosophy of employee-hiring represents a practical application of the findings confirmed in our study. It explains, perhaps, why the strong-willed man or woman typically gets off to a slower start in business than the more compliant individual. Bosses and supervisors want employees who will follow instructions and avoid hassles with coworkers. Incidentally, in another study of people who were fired from their places of employment, fewer than 20 percent lost their jobs for the lack of technical knowledge and skill. More than 80 percent were released because of their inability to get along with *people*. That is their Achilles heel, despite their aptitude for a particular kind of work. Thus, the easygoing young man or woman has a distinct advantage in early positions of employment. That is precisely what we found.

But let me speculate about how this picture might change with the passage of time. Since our study was limited to those individuals twenty-four years of age and younger, I have wondered what happens to those who are forty and older. It is my supposition that strong-willed individuals will eventually emerge as the entrepreneurs and leaders. Their desire for independence and their aggressive temperaments might cause them to outproduce their compliant counterparts in the long run.

My good friend, Dr. Malcolm Williamson, whom I referred to earlier, has assessed the personality traits of thousands of adults in the work force. His research shows clearly that corporation presidents are characteristically dominant (strong-willed), aggressive, self-confident, fast-paced, and highly independent. Conversely, he finds a high percentage of vice presidents and middlemanagement executives are "servants." They carry out company policy very well. They tend to be loyal, dedicated perfectionists who do not want to be wrong. And yes, they tend to be compliant.

I believe our study would have confirmed these findings if we had extended the time frame for two more decades. Perhaps we will do so some day.

Conclusion

Now that I have thoroughly depressed the parents of very strong-willed children, let me make two summarizing comments and offer a few encouraging thoughts.

First, there was another finding from our study which should provide hope to every mother and father on the battlefield today. It concerns the return to parental values by these most difficult individuals when they reach adulthood. Depicted on the chart below is what we were told by 853 parents:

Table 5—Acceptance or Rejection of Parental Values

	Accepted Parental Values	Rejected Parental Values	Somewhat Accepted Parental Values
Very compliant children, now grown	79%	5%	15%
Very strong-willed children, now grown	53%	15%	32%
Total	60%	12%	32%

As can be observed, 53 percent of even the most strong-willed and rebellious children eventually return to the values of their parents, outright. When that figure is combined with those who are "somewhat" accepting of parental perspectives, that means 85 percent of these hardheaded, independent individuals will eventually lean toward their parents' point of view by the time adolescence is over. Only 15 percent are so headstrong that they reject everything their family stood for, and I'll wager that there were other problems and sources of pain in most of those cases.

What this means, in effect, is that these tough-minded kids will fuss and fight and complain throughout their years at home, but the majority will turn around as young adults and do what their parents most desired. Remember, also, that there was a category of individuals whom we described as "rather strong-willed," who have not been considered in any of these analyses. It is virtually certain that the percentage of these less antagonistic kids who accept parental values is higher than those represented above. It is also reassuring to know, in this context, that even the *most* defiant individuals who go through awful rebellion in adolescence are likely to come back to parental values . . . partially if not entirely. Furthermore, if we could evaluate these individuals at thirty-five instead of twenty-four years of age, even fewer would still be in rebellion against parental values.

Second, I urge you as parents of strong-willed children not to feel "cheated" or depressed by the assignment of raising such individuals. All human beings arrive with a generous assortment of flaws, including the very compliant child. Yes, it is more difficult to raise an independent little fellow, but you can do it! You can, through prayer and supplication before the Lord, bring him to that period of harmony in early adulthood that makes the effort worthwhile. I also believe that you can increase the odds of transmitting your values to these individuals by following some time-honored principles which we will discuss. So hang in there! Nothing of any real value in life comes easy anyway, except the free gift of salvation from Jesus Christ.

Let's look now, in chapter 4, at the ways parents react to defiant and compliant children. You might find your own reflection somewhere in the discussion that follows.

Chapter Four

What 35,000 Parents said about Themselves

You will recall from the first chapter that many parents told us they were *intensely* frustrated by their child-rearing responsibilities. More than 30 percent responding to our survey said, in effect, "I am a failure as a parent!" and "I simply can't cope with my kids." But who are these mothers and fathers who have felt such despair at home? I believe we now have revealing answers to that and other important questions.

The thirty-five thousand parents who participated in our study not only gave us valuable information about their strongwilled and compliant children (reported in chapter 3), but they also described their own feelings and attitudes about raising them. Their responses were surprising in many contexts. Let's look at a few of the more relevant findings, some of which were alarming.

One of the items on the questionnaire (see Appendix) asked parents to rate the amount of stress that was created by their children's temperaments. Then we divided the sample to compare the responses of parents of very

PARENTING ISN'T FOR COWARDS

compliant children vs. those of the very strong-willed. This is what we found:

Table 6—Parental Response to Strong-willed and Compliant Children

	Total Joy	Generally Pleasant	Average	Generally Difficult	Unpleasant
Parents of very compliant children	44%	51%	4%	1%	0%
Parents of very strong-willed children	1%	10%	17%	55%	17%

What a dramatic story these statistics tell. If we combine the two positive categories (total joy and generally pleasant), we find that 95 percent of parents raising very compliant children felt good about the job they were doing, compared with only 11 percent of the parents of strong-willed children. On the negative side, 1 percent of the parents of compliant children rated the assignment generally difficult or unpleasant, compared with 72 percent of those raising strong-willed kids. Obviously, we have identified the bulk of frustrated parents from this one item on our questionnaire.

A second item was intended to explore further the reactions of parents to children with easy or difficult personalities. We asked for this information: "Generally speaking, select the sentence that best describes how you feel about raising your very strong-willed or very compliant children." The four alternative statements were:

1. "It has been a struggle that has often left me depressed, guilt-ridden, and exhausted."
2. "It has been difficult but exciting and rewarding too."
3. "It has been a very positive experience."

Parents of strong-willed children were then given this fourth choice:

4. "He/she was difficult in the early years, but the adolescent years were less stormy and difficult."

Parents of compliant children were then given this fourth choice:

4. "He/she was a joy in the early years, but adolescence was extremely stressful for both generations."

Having obtained responses from 4,801 parents, we divided the sample into eight subgroups in an attempt to identify the parents in greatest distress. We were looking at both strong-willed and compliant mothers and fathers as they interacted with their very strong-willed and very compliant children. The findings are provided in Table 7 (see next page).

Even a cursory examination of these responses makes it clear that strong-willed children are a source of great frustration not only to their mothers, which we expected, but also to their fathers. Lynn Caine, writing in her book *What Did I Do Wrong?*, said this about men: ". . . fathers . . . seemed not to share either the guilt or the blame . . . They did not feel hated or inadequate or responsible for them. *That* was for women to feel . . . I have seldom met a guilty father . . . Perhaps our guilt is a condition of womankind, a weakness of the sex, the natural softness of the nurturer."[1]

According to our findings, Mrs. Caine is wrong. Fathers *do* struggle when their children rebel. This fact is verified by adding the first two columns to create what might be called a "negative factor," appearing in the middle column. This combined percentage shows that strong-willed children not only affect mothers and fathers equally, but they create about the same degree of stress for strong-willed and compliant parents. The lowest positive rating (4 percent) occurred for very compliant fathers raising very strong-willed children. In short, every adult who works with these rambunctious youngsters is affected by the tension they create! We will come back to this point in a moment.

Let's turn our attention now from how parents *feel* to how they *discipline*. Some equally dramatic findings turned up at this point. Our primary interest was in the handling of very strong-willed vs. very compliant children. We asked those completing the questionnaire to indicate which parent related best to the children at various age levels. Table 8 depicts the response of parents to very strong-willed children only.

From this analysis and several dozen others, it was apparent that mothers of strong-willed children are especially vulnerable to their rebellious kids. As indicated earlier, fathers also struggle and feel guilty in reference to them. Nevertheless, men appear willing to accept an increasing share of the child-rearing responsibility with the passage of time. Mothers begin in complete charge of their young children, handling 78 percent of their strong-willed toddlers. From there, they slide downhill in

Table 7

Parent-Child Interactions According to Temperaments of Both Generations

Parent/Child Temperaments	1 Struggle	2 Difficult	Negative Factor (1 and 2 Combined)	3 Positive	4 Variable
Very compliant mothers with very compliant children	3%	11%	14%	71%	15%
Very compliant mothers with very strong-willed children	43%	44%	87%	6%	7%
Strong-willed mothers with compliant children	5%	13%	18%	64%	18%
Strong-willed mothers with strong-willed children	34%	56%	90%	6%	4%
Very compliant fathers with very compliant children	3%	14%	17%	71%	12%
Very compliant fathers with very strong-willed children	41%	50%	91%	4%	5%
Very strong-willed fathers with very compliant children	6%	12%	18%	65%	17%
Very strong-willed fathers with very strong-willed children	39%	51%	90%	6%	4%

Number of Parents Polled:

Very compliant mothers	980
Very compliant fathers	710
Very strong-willed mothers	1,684
Very strong-willed fathers	1,427
Totals	4,801

every age category through adolescence. Fathers actually related to the greater percentage of individuals between thirteen and twenty years of age by a few percentage points. A rebound then occurs in young adulthood, favoring mothers again. We are assuming that this transfer of parenting responsibilities from women to men occurs because mothers dislike confrontation and are less comfortable than fathers with the power games played by these tougher sons and daughters.

Table 8—Who Handles Strong-Willed Children Best?

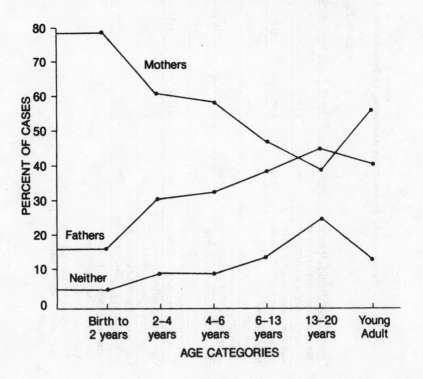

Of greater significance in this context is the bottom line of the graph, showing the percentage of children to whom *neither* parent related very well. The peak of 24 percent of cases in the adolescent years spells trouble! One-fourth of all tough-minded youngsters do not get along well with *either* mother or father, and 14 percent are still charting their own course in young adulthood. Like their parents, these are the teens who desperately need outside influence of the right type.

When responses to the question, "Who handles the child best?" were plotted by sex, it was noted that fathers carry an even greater responsibility for strong-willed sons than they do with their daughters. Surprisingly, however, girls were just as rebellious as boys during adolescence.

Let's compare responses, now, from parents of very compliant children. The pattern is dramatically different.

It does not require a statistician to draw meaning from these data. Clearly, mothers love compliant children. Fathers are fond of them, too, but Mom is in the driver's seat throughout childhood. Notice the small percentage of compliant children who feel alienated from both parents (a maximum of 5 percent during adolescence).

Upon seeing these figures for the first time, a struggling mother of a strong-willed tribe said to me wearily, "Where do I get some of those compliant kids?!" I don't know, but the chances are great that *her* parents would also have wanted that information.

From the outset of this study I was especially interested in the relationship between mothers and their daughters. Many psychologists have described a so-called "thing" which seemingly occurs between females

51

Table 9—Who Handles Compliant Children Best?

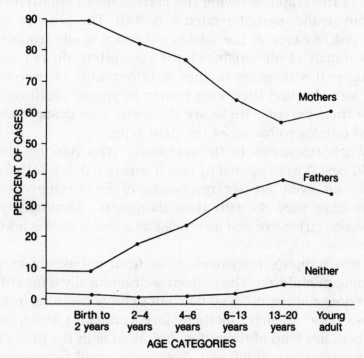

in the same house. Whether it is a phenomenon of "two women in the kitchen" or a natural competitiveness for the attention of the husband/father, there does seem to be some validity to it. It is not unusual for a mother to say during this period, "I don't like either my son *or* my daughter right now." Evidences of such difficulties were found in our study. For example, only 36 percent of mothers related best to their strong-willed daughters during adolescence. Conflict was evident in the remaining two-thirds of the cases. Other examples of that antagonism were also unearthed in our study.

Another interesting factor was noted regarding mothers' and fathers' discipline. Parents were asked to rate themselves as permissive, rather easy, average, rather strict or rigid/severe. We then cross-tabulated that rating against children's social success at various ages. They were categorized as having no problems, generally liked, average, generally disliked, and having many problems. This is what we found: For the children with many problems, their parents tended to be either permissive with them or they were rigid/severe. The pattern held through many analyses and at virtually each age category from childhood to adulthood. The conclusion is that when children are beset by major social problems, their parents react in extreme ways—either by throwing up their hands and refusing to discipline them at all, or by becoming so rigid and severe as to oppress them. This analysis and several others made it clear that the kind of discipline a parent applies is a function of the child's well-being and of his temperament. When he is unusually difficult or beset by numerous problems, parenting effectiveness sometimes suffers accordingly.

Summary

As indicated earlier, I could fill many books with the massive amount of information generated from this study of thirty-five thousand parents. Admittedly, this was a *retrospective* investigation instead of a more scientific *longitudinal* effort. Nevertheless, the findings speak for themselves. The gap between strong-willed and compliant children is indeed a chasm, and those differences in temperament and behavior have a dramatic effect on those who are raising them.

PARENTING ISN'T FOR COWARDS

Perhaps it is now evident why I am especially concerned about the four groups of parents raising very strong-willed children (see Table 7 again). I believe many of these mothers and fathers are near the breaking point today. Their sense of guilt is overwhelming, and yet they have typically carried their pain in silence. I would expect the incidences of child abuse, child abandonment, parental alcoholism and other evidences of family disintegration to be inordinately high in this category. And of course, it is not a category or a group at all. I'm talking about real *people*—living, breathing mothers and fathers who are going down for the count.

If you are one of those struggling parents who has wept in the midnight hours, the balance of this book is for you. While we will also address the special problems encountered by compliant children, the greater urgency must be on the rebellious individual and his family. There is hope for him and for you, his parents.

[1] Lyn Caine, *What Did I Do Wrong? Mothers, Children, Guilt* (New York: Arbor House, 1985), 136.

Chapter Five

With Love to Parents Who Hurt

Some time ago, I attended a wedding ceremony held in a beautiful garden setting. After the minister instructed the groom to kiss his bride, approximately 150 colorful, helium-filled balloons were released into the blue California sky. It was a pleasant sight that reminded me of a similar moment during the 1984 Olympics in Los Angeles. Within a few seconds, the balloons were scattered across the heavens—some rising hundreds of feet overhead and others cruising toward the horizon. The distribution was curious. They all began from a common launching pad, were filled with approximately the same amount of helium, and ascended into the same conditions of sun and wind. Nevertheless, within a matter of several minutes they were separated by a mile or more. A few balloons struggled to clear the upper branches of trees, while the show-offs became mere pinpoints of color on their journey to the sky. How interesting, I thought—and how symbolic of children.

We have already agreed that babies do not begin life's

journey from a common launching pad. They also vary in their ability to fly. Let's face it. Some carry more helium than others. But even if they were identical at birth, they would not remain equivalent for long. Environmental influences would carry them in infinite directions within the span of a few days. From that point forward, they only drift farther apart. Some kids seem to catch all the right breezes. They soar effortlessly to the heights. Their parents beam with pride for having created superior balloons. Others wobble dangerously close to the trees. Their frantic folks run along underneath, huffing and puffing to keep them airborne. It is an exhausting experience.

I want to offer a word of encouragement at this point to the parents of every low-flying kid in the world today. There's usually one or more in each family. They're not all strong-willed and rebellious, of course. Some are physically handicapped. Others have learning disabilities or peculiar personalities or serious illnesses. Some have other characteristics that bring ridicule from their peers. What is it that worries you about your different child? Is he overweight or underweight or very short or tall or clumsy or lazy? Or is he so terribly selfish and unpleasant that he has alienated everyone he's met except (or including) you? Is the story of your family written somewhere within the flight plan of your "special balloon"?

May I gently put my arm around you through the pages of this book? I understand your pain and your fears. Your hopes rise and fall with the altitude of this different youngster. You awaken in the wee hours of the morning, worrying and praying for his survival. You have nightmares that his balloon will go into a frantic loop-the-loop and then plunge in a power dive to the earth.

You would give your life to prevent this catastrophe, but that wouldn't help. You're all he has.

If you've launched only high-flying sons and daughters, then you won't comprehend the sentiment of these words. You may even think them foolish. It is very difficult to understand the depression and apprehension that can accompany the rearing of such a child unless you've been through it. It is also embarrassing. Why? Because of the crazy notion that parents are responsible for everything their child becomes. They are praised or blamed for his successes and failures—all of them. If he is gorgeous, brilliant, artistic, athletic, scholarly, and polite, his folks get an A+ for having made him that way. But if he is ordinary, uncoordinated, indolent, homely, unpleasant and dull, they fail the course. Mom and Dad are particularly accountable for their child's misbehavior, even years after he is beyond their control or influence. I hear from parents almost every day who share stories similar to this one:

> Dear Dr. Dobson:
>
> We have four children including a boy and girl in college. They are doing beautifully and have become everything parents dream of. We also have a twelve-year-old boy whose brain was damaged at birth. He's a beautiful child who works extremely hard to keep his head above water. Finally, we have a thirteen-year-old boy who has been strong-willed from "day one," as you often say.
>
> We've been Christians for seven years, and we've done everything possible to help this child—from prayer, to moving this past year, to putting him in a Christian school, to weekly family counseling sessions.

Tonight we had to sit with our son in front of the pastor, the minister of education, and members of the Christian school board to request that he not be kicked out of school with only six weeks left. The verdict: He's out! The comment was made by the minister of education to this effect, "What kind of parents are you not to have more control over your son?"

We are desperate! Everything we can think of has been tried with this child. We love him dearly but I sure see why parents abuse their children. I'm an X-ray technician and I see too many brain-damaged children from abuse. Maybe at this moment that is what keeps me from beating him. But why do these school administrators put more guilt on us when people like you try so hard to help us handle it? We have enough guilt already, knowing that we are failures at parenting.

Please help. We are desperate!

God bless you,
Elaine

If we talked to the school board and the minister of education, we might hear a different story about these parents and their rebellious son. Perhaps they did cause his defiant behavior, but I doubt it. When we look at their other children we see they are doing fine. No, I think the parents are victims of the cruel misunderstanding of which we have spoken. They and other contemporary parents have been taught that children are born neutral and good. If the children go wrong, it is because someone wreaks havoc upon them. All behavior is *caused*, say the experts. The child chooses nothing. He merely responds to his experiences.

As indicated earlier, this theory is called *determinism*, and if it is valid, then the responsibility for every lie, every school failure, every act of defiance eventually circles around to his family—especially to his mother. This is why she has been blamed for all the problems and even the silly imperfections that beset her children. Is it any wonder that one thousand mothers and fathers who responded to our "frustrations of parenthood poll" gave as their most common answer, "I am a failure as a parent"?

I remember boarding a commercial airliner a few years ago on a trip from Los Angeles to Toronto. No sooner had I become comfortable than a mother sat down two seats from me and promptly placed her three-year-old son between us. *Oh boy!* I thought. *I get to spend five hours strapped next to this little livewire.* I expected him to drive his mother and me crazy by the time we landed. If my son Ryan had been strapped in a chair at that age and given nothing to do, he would have dismantled the entire tail section of the plane by the time it landed. My father once said about Ryan, "If you allow that kid to become bored, you *deserve* what he will do to you."

To my surprise, the toddler next to me sat pleasantly for five long hours. He sang little songs. He played with the ashtray. For an hour or two he slept. But mostly, he engaged himself in thought. I kept expecting him to claw the air, but it never happened. His mother was not surprised. She acted as though all three-year-olds were able to sit for half a day with nothing interesting to do.

Contrast that uneventful episode with another flight I took a few months later. I boarded a plane, found my seat, and glanced to my left. Seated across from me this time was a well-dressed woman and a *very* ambitious two-year-old girl. Correction! The mother was seated but her daughter was most definitely not. This little girl had no intention of sitting down—or slowing down. It was also obvious that the mother did not have control of the child, and indeed, Superman himself might have had difficulty harnessing her. The toddler shouted "No!" every few seconds as her mother tried to rein her in. If Mom persisted she would scream at the top of her lungs while kicking and lunging to escape. I looked at my watch and thought, *What is this poor woman going to do when she is required to buckle that kid in her seat?*

I could see that the mother was accustomed to losing these major confrontations with her daughter. Obviously, the child was used to winning. That arrangement might have achieved a tentative peace at home or in a restaurant, but this was different. They were faced with a situation on the plane where the mother *couldn't* give in. To have allowed the child to roam during takeoff would have been dangerous and impermissible under FAA regulations. Mom *had* to win—perhaps for the first time ever.

In a few minutes, the flight attendant came by and urged the mother to buckle the child down. Easy for her to say! I will never forget what occurred in the next few minutes. The two-year-old threw a tantrum that must have set some kind of international record for violence and expended energy. She was kicking, sobbing, screaming, and writhing for freedom! Twice she tore loose from her mom's arms and scurried toward the aisle. The mortified woman was literally begging her child to settle down and cooperate. Everyone in our section of the plane was embarrassed for the humiliated mother. Those of us within ten feet were also virtually deaf by that point.

Finally, the plane taxied down the runway and took off with the mother hanging onto this thrashing toddler with all her strength. Once we were airborne, she was able at last to release the little fireball. When the crisis was over, the mother covered her face with both hands and wept. I felt her pain too.

Why didn't I help her? Because my advice would have offended the mother. The child desperately needed the security of strong parental leadership at that moment, but the woman had no idea how to provide it. A few sharp slaps on the legs would probably have taken some of the fire out of her. The affair could have ended with a sleeping child curled in her mother's loving arms. Instead, it set the stage for even more violent and costly confrontations in the years ahead.

It is interesting to speculate on how the mothers on these two airplanes probably felt about themselves and their very different toddlers. I would guess that the woman with the passive little boy was significantly over-confident. Raising kids for her was duck soup. "You tell 'em what to do and expect 'em to do it!" she could have said. Some mothers in her comfortable situation hold unconcealed disdain for parents of rebellious children. They just can't understand why others find child-rearing so difficult.

The mother of the second toddler, on the other hand, was almost certainly experiencing a great crisis of confidence. I could see it in her eyes. She wondered how she had managed to make such a mess of parenting in two short years! Somehow, she had taken a precious newborn baby and twisted her into a monster. But how did it happen? What did she do to cause such outrageous behavior? She may ask those questions for the rest of her life.

I wish she had known that at least part of the problem resided in the temperament of the child. It was her nature to grab for power, and the mother was making a serious mistake by granting it to her.

This is my point: Parents today are much too willing to blame themselves for everything their children (or adolescents) do. Only in this century have they been so inclined. If a kid went bad one hundred years ago, he was a bad kid. Now it's the fault of his parents. Admittedly, many mothers and fathers *do* warp and twist their children during the vulnerable years. I am not pleading their cases. Believe me, I know that our society today is peppered with terrible parents who don't care about their kids. Some are addicted to alcohol, gambling, pedophilia, pornography, or just plain selfishness. This book is not written to soothe their guilt. But there are others who care passionately about their sons and daughters and they do the best they can to raise them properly. Nevertheless, when their kids entangle themselves in sin and heartache, guess who feels reponsible for it? Behavior is caused, isn't it? The blame inevitably makes a sweeping U-turn and lodges itself in the hearts of the parents.

I am particularly concerned about the mother and father who give the highest priority to the task of parenthood. Their firstborn child is conceived in love and born in great joy. They will neither talk nor think of much else for the next three years. The first smile; the first word;

the first birthday; the first step. Every milestone is a cause for celebration. They buy him a tricycle and they teach him to fly a kite. And they patch up the bird with the broken wing. Only the best will do for this inheritor of the family name. They buy him Child-Craft® books and teach him to sing. They show him how to pray. It is a labor of love that knows no limits.

Before they know it, their precious little lad is ready for kindergarten. How time flies! They buy him new clothes and cut his hair and get him a Snoopy lunch pail. "Hurry, now," says his mom on the first day of school. "Let's don't be late." She walks with him across the street and waits for the big yellow bus that stops on the corner. It arrives presently and the door opens. She places the child on the first step and then moves backward to take his picture. The door closes and the bus rumbles slowly down the street. Mom watches as long as it is in sight and then she turns toward her house. She cries quietly as she crosses the street. Her baby is growing up.

The years pass so quickly but it is a happy time. The boy learns to ride a bicycle and soon he's heavily into bugs and snakes and spiders. He gives Little League a try and Dad attends every game. You'd think it was the World Series! There is nothing this father would not do for his son. The boy loves his mom and dad, too, although he has a mind of his own. He has always been somewhat assertive and independent. His cousins think he is a brat. Some of the church folks think he is spoiled. His parents think he's just immature. All three are right.

The tenth, eleventh, and twelfth years are marked by

increasing tension in the house, but major blowups have not yet occurred. Then, suddenly, the roof falls in. The boy turns thirteen and a dramatic change settles over him. Overnight, almost, he has become distant and edgy. He explodes whenever he is frustrated, which seems to happen every few days. He also resents his parents for the first time. He shrinks back when they touch him and he objects to the pet names they have always used. He hates his mom's cooking and complains about the way she irons his shirts. It is a very tough year.

At fourteen, he spends long hours in his room with his door closed. Because life has become intolerable at home he talks vaguely about running away. His parents are utterly bewildered. What did they do? How have they changed? They feel no different, yet this son whom they love so much has targeted them as his enemies. Why? They are hurt and confused.

When he is fifteen, Mom is cleaning his room one day and finds some weird-looking cigarettes behind a bookend. "Could it be? Would he really? Oh no! Not our son!" Then they discover a bottle of little red pills in the bottom drawer of his dresser. "Where is he getting the money?"

Every day is a struggle now for his mother and father. He will not yield to their leadership. This young man, whom they have cherished, seems bent on destroying himself before he is grown. He comes home at all hours of the night reeking of alcohol and smoke. If they demand to know where he's been, he blows up. "Get off my back!" he screams. They are worried sick.

Dad talks to the juvenile authorities on the phone. "I

just can't control him," he says. "Sorry," the officer replies,"there's nothing we can do until he commits a serious crime. Even then we can be of little help. There are so many . . . . "

At sixteen, the boy buys himself a car. Now he is really emancipated. His folks rarely see him. He fails four classes as a sophomore and quits school as a junior. From there to his nineteenth year, he is involved in three automobile accidents, gets seven tickets for speeding, and finally, is arrested for driving under the influence. He spends a night in the tank for that one, which nearly kills his mother. Dad's car insurance policy is summarily cancelled.

Now, at twenty, he's living with a girl who is not his wife. She had an abortion last year and is pregnant again. They fight continually over money. He's never held a job for more than three months and they're living on food stamps and State assistance. A friend tells his parents that their son is snorting cocaine now.

Most painful of all to his mother and father is his rejection of their faith. He says he hates their religion and never accepted a word of it. "You can believe what you want," he sneers, "but don't try to sell it to me." Long-term, unrelenting depression settles over their home like a thick black cloud.

Does this frightening scenario actually occur in solid, secure, loving Christian homes? Yes, occasionally it does. And when it happens to *you* and your family, it might as well be a worldwide plague. I feel great tenderness toward parents who have been there. One of them, a mother of three grown daughters, wrote to me recently. This is what she said:

PARENTING ISN'T FOR COWARDS

Dear Dr. Dobson:

Your radio interview with Dr. John White was so helpful. I had already read his book, *Parents in Pain*, but it ministered to me again. [Incidentally, I recommend this book highly to my readers.]

We have three daughters, ages 20, 23, and 24, raised as well as we could do it. I read Kesler and I read Trobisch. I did the best I could to be a good example and to follow Christian standards. I spent hours trying to show them that each one was valued and loved immensely. I tried to give them room to be individuals and we both enjoyed watching them develop into adults. In our zeal we never even bought a TV set!!!

Results: we have two daughters who couldn't have turned out better and one who couldn't have turned out worse. Our oldest daughter is a college graduate, has a productive job, is loving her Christian walk and is a joy to have around.

Daughter #3 caused us untold grief and worry and finally at age 18 ran off with a 29-year-old thrice-married ex-convict (who was still married to wife #3). For 3 weeks I sat at the kitchen table all day in shock.

I didn't know that anyone could endure that much pain and still live. At first I thought I would commit suicide. Then I thought I would go around forever with FAILURE branded on my forehead. My husband and I had long discussions about whether we should drop out of the church and not attempt to minister to others because of our failure. It shook our marriage to the roots. We felt like 26 years went down the drain. It was so embarrassing to see people who knew what had happened. It was worse to run into people who didn't know, because they might ask how our girls were. I would cut people absolutely dead so they wouldn't have a chance to ask.

I complained to God for "letting it happen." For many weeks I considered giving up the Christian walk, but on the other hand I could hardly wait for church and the Bible study because of the help I knew was there. Finally I did come to the point where I had to admit to God that I had to stick with Him because only He had the words of eternal life, but I could hardly pray for months because my heart was like a rock.

Now, almost exactly two years have passed. We finally know where she is, and only this week she has decided that she would even write us a letter.

There is a special group of parents at church who have formed an unspoken brotherhood because their children have broken their hearts, and other parents with all good kids lightly compare notes while the rest of us sit silently with aching hearts.

I tell you, Dr. Dobson, that it would be easier to bury the children than it would be to see them using their bodies for such shameful purposes—those bodies that we've lovingly washed, bandaged, dressed, stuffed good food and vitamins into, kept out of the lake, and off of the roads—using their lives to advance the cause of Satan. I sincerely hope that *you* never hear your kid say, "I hate you. You've ruined my life and I never want to see you again," and walk out coolly.

I want to tell you something else about the effect this has had on our family that we didn't expect. Our oldest daughter says: "I will never have any children." Parents spend years doing their best for the children, and suddenly at age 14 the parents become despised enemies. I refuse to put up with that for myself."

I could go on for several more paragraphs, but I think you get the idea, as much as you could, not having gone through it yourself.

God bless you. Keep up the good work.

Sincerely,
Mary Alice

This mother was right. I have never experienced the kind of pain she has described, for which I'm grateful. But I believe I understand it. I have witnessed the same trauma in hundreds of families. It is one of the most devastating experiences in living. Most of the parents I have known who are dealing with adolescent or postadolescent rebellion respond precisely as Mary Alice did. They blame themselves. Note that she felt as though the word "failure" had been branded across her forehead. She was so humiliated she contemplated suicide. She and her husband thought of dropping out of church because they considered themselves no longer worthy as Christians. These are the words of guilt-ridden parents who have believed the great lie. In their minds, they had destroyed their own precious daughter. They were convinced that even God could not forgive so great a sin.

Guilt is one of the most painful emotions in human experience. Sometimes it is valid and represents the displeasure of God Himself. When that is the case, it can be forgiven and forgotten. On other occasions, it is entirely of our own creation. Mary Alice and her husband appear to be victims of this self-imposed condemnation, as are thousands of other parents. As with the writer of the earlier letter, this mother and her husband had raised three girls by the same philosophy and technique. If they were such horrid parents, why did two daughters turn out so well? I believe the vast differences between these three young women is traceable more to their own temperaments and choices than to the successes and failures of their parents. Nevertheless, Mary Alice felt totally responsible for the mess her youngest daughter was in. It wasn't fair. But that's the way mothers are made.

This tendency to assume the responsibility for everything our teenagers and grown children do is not only a product of psychological mumbo-jumbo (determinism) but it reflects our own vulnerabilities as parents. We know we are flawed. We know how often we fail. Even under the best of circumstances, we are forced time after time to guess at what is right for our children. Errors in judgment occur. Then our own selfishness surfaces and we do and say things that can never be undone. All these shortcomings are then magnified tenfold when a son or daughter goes bad.

Finally, the inclination toward self-condemnation also reflects the way Christians have been taught to believe. Though I am not a theologian, it is apparent to me that a serious misunderstanding of several key passages has occurred. The error has produced false condemnation for circumstances that exceed parental control or influence.

Consider, for example, the pastor who wrote me in anguish after his twenty-one-year-old son impregnated his girlfriend on a Christian college campus. The minister was devastated. He felt as guilty as though he had personally been caught in an adulterous affair. This anguished man, who was a successful and popular pastor, wrote a letter of confession to his church and resigned as their leader. He cited Titus 1:6 as evidence of his unworthiness to continue in the ministry.

The verse he quoted is a portion of the apostle Paul's statement of qualifications for church leadership. Paul said a bishop must be "the husband of but one wife, a man whose children believe and are not open to the charge of being wild and disobedient." You may draw your own conclusions from this scripture, but I believe it refers to much younger children than the pastor's son. This young man was twenty-one years of age and had gone away to college. He was no longer a child!

Remember, also, that males and females were considered grown much earlier in Paul's day. They often married between fourteen to sixteen years of age. Thus, when Paul referred to a man having his children in proper subjection, I believe he was talking about *children*. He intended to disqualify men who had chaotic families and those who were unable to discipline or manage their young sons and daughters. That is a far cry from holding a man responsible for the rebellious behavior of his grown offspring, or in this instance, for a single sinful event. They are beyond his control.

The pastor who wrote to me might take solace from reading again the book of Genesis. It would appear that God Himself would not qualify for Church leadership according to the pastor's interpretation of Titus 1:6, because His wayward "children," Adam and Eve, fell into sin. Obviously, in my view, something is wrong with this interpretation of the Scriptures.

Ezekiel 18 is also helpful to us in assessing blame for

the sinful behavior of grown children. God's way ing at that situation is abundantly clear:

> The word of the Lord came to me: "What do you peo
> mean by quoting this proverb about the land of Isra
> 'The fathers eat sour grapes, and the children's te
> are set on edge'?
>
> As surely as I live, declares the Sovereign Lord, y
> will no longer quote this proverb in Israel. For every
> ing soul belongs to me, the father as well as the sor
> both alike belong to me. The soul who sins is the c
> who will die" (Ezekiel 18:1–4).

Then in verse 20 he concludes: "The son will no the guilt of the father, nor will the father share th of the son. The righteousness of the righteous man credited to him, and the wickedness of the wicked charged against him."

These words from the Lord should end the contr once and for all. Each adult is responsible for hi behavior, and that of no one else.

So where does this leave us as Christian parent we without spiritual resources with which to suppo sons and daughters? Absolutely not! We are give powerful weapon of intercessory prayer which never be underestimated. The Scriptures teach th can pray effectively for one another and that such a tion "availeth much" (James 5:16, KJV). God's answ our request will not remove the freedom of choice our children, but He will grant them clarity and u standing in charting their own course. They will be every opportunity to make the right decisions rega matters of eternal significance. I also believe the Lor

place key individuals in the paths of the ones for whom we pray—people of influence who can nudge them in the right direction.

Shirley and I prayed this prayer for our son and daughter throughout their developmental years: "Be here, Father, in the moment of decision when two paths present themselves to our children. Especially during that time when they are beyond our direct influence, send others who will help them do what is righteous and just."

I believe God honors and answers that kind of intercessory prayer. I learned that from my grandmother, who seemed to live in the presence of God. She had prayed for her six children throughout their formative years, but her youngest son (my father) was a particularly headstrong young man. For seven years following his high school graduation, he had left the church and rejected its teachings. Then, as it happened, an evangelist came to town and a great spiritual awakening swept their local church. But my father would have no part of it and refused even to attend.

One evening as the rest of the family was preparing to go to church, my father (who was visiting his parents' home) slipped away and hid on the side porch. He could hear his brothers chatting as they boarded the car. Then one of them, Willis, said suddenly, "Hey, where's Jim? Isn't he going tonight?"

Someone else said, "No, Willis. He said he isn't ever going to church again."

My father heard his brother get out of the car and begin searching for him all over the house. Willis had experienced a personal relationship with Jesus Christ when he was nine years old and he loved the Lord passionately. He

had held tightly to his faith throughout adolescence when his brothers (including my father) mocked him unmercifully. They had called him "Preacher Boy," "Sissy," and "Goody-Goody." It only made him more determined to do what was right.

My dad remained silent as Willis hurried through the house calling his name. Finally, he found his brother sitting silently in the swing on the side porch.

"Jim," he said, "aren't you going with us to the service tonight?"

My dad said, "No, Willis. I'm through with all of that. I don't plan to ever go back again."

Willis said nothing. But as my father sat looking at the floor, he saw big tears splashing on his brother's shoes. My father was deeply moved that Willis would love him that much, after the abuse he had taken for his Christian stand.

I'll go just because it means that much to him, my dad said to himself.

Because of the delay my father had caused, the family was late arriving at the church that night. The only seats left were on the second row from the front. They streamed down the aisle and were seated. A song evangelist was singing and the words began to speak to my dad's heart. Just that quickly, he yielded. After seven years of rebellion and sin, it was over. He was forgiven. He was clean.

The evangelist at that time was a man named Bona Fleming, who was unusually anointed of God. When the singer concluded, Reverend Fleming walked across the platform and put his foot on the altar rail. He leaned forward and pointed his finger directly at my dad.

"You! Young man! Right there! Stand up!"

My father rose to his feet.

"Now, I want you to tell all these people what God did for you while the singer was singing!"

My dad gave his first testimony, through his tears, of the forgiveness and salvation he had just received. Willis was crying too. So was my grandmother. She had prayed for him unceasingly for more than seven years.

To the day of his death at sixty-six years of age, my father never wavered from that decision. His only passion was to serve the God with whom he fell in love during a simple hymn. But where would he have been if Willis had not gone to look for him? How different life would have been for him . . . and for me. God answered the prayers of my grandmother by putting a key person at the critical crossroads.

He will do as much for your children, too, if you keep them in your prayers. But until that moment comes, pray for them in *confidence*—not in regret. The past is the past. You can't undo your mistakes. You could no more be a perfect parent than you could be a perfect human being. Let your guilt do the work God intended and then file it away forever. I'll bet Solomon would agree with that advice.

Chapter Six

Suggestions for Parents of Young Children

The best way to deal with parental guilt, of course, is to prevent it from occurring in the first place. We've taken a step in that direction by exposing false guilt resulting from circumstances beyond our control. But we must not go too far in that direction. Parents are accountable before God to meet their responsibilities to their children, and He is vitally concerned about their welfare. Jesus said that anyone who would hurt the faith of a little child would be better off sinking in the sea with a millstone attached to his neck. That warning is relevant to us as mothers and fathers. Our failure to love and discipline our children often inflicts upon them a weak and damaged faith. There is no greater tragedy in life!

We also want to do our best for our kids because we love them dearly. In that spirit, then, let me offer a few suggestions to parents of babies and children who have not yet reached their thirteenth birthdays.

1. Go with the Flow

I took my son Ryan and one of his friends on a ski trip when they were about twelve years of age. As we rode the gondola to the top of the mountain, I decided to snap the boys' picture with the beautiful scenery visible behind them. While I focused the shot, Ryan began clowning and waving at the camera. Ricky, on the other hand, sat glumly and quietly beside him.

"Come on, Rick!" said Ryan. "Loosen up! Smile for the camera!"

Ricky never changed his expression but simply said dryly, "I'm not that kind of person."

He was right. Ricky is reserved and dignified while Ryan is spontaneous and flamboyant. It's the way they are constructed. In a thousand years of practice Ricky could not be like Ryan, and Ryan would come unstitched if he had to be as controlled as Ricky. It was interesting to see how the boys recognized and accepted their differences in basic temperaments.

A surprising degree of diversity can occur even between children born to the same parents. For example, there were five boys in my father's family. The oldest two were twins who developed into great athletes. One went on to coach football at Byrd High School in Shreveport, Louisiana. The next eldest was Willis, who wore thick glasses and could neither catch nor throw a ball. He earned a Ph.D. in Shakespearean literature at the University of Texas and then taught college English for forty-five years.

The next in line was a gifted businessman who saved part of every dollar he ever earned. He was president of two Coca-Cola® bottling plants when he died.

Finally, there was my dad—a sensitive artist by desire and a minister by the calling of God. With the exception of the twins, these brothers could not have been more unique if they had come from four different families. My father didn't even look like his brothers, being 6' 4" tall while the others were 5' 9" or less. Obviously, God had taken a common genetic pool and fashioned five unique and distinct individuals from it.

Some of my readers might be wondering if we are absolutely sure that my grandfather was really the sire of this crew, but there's no doubt about that. I am reminded, however, of a man who lay dying and called his wife to his bedside. He then turned to her and said, "Mildred, I've always wanted to ask you about the youngest of our twelve children. He just doesn't look like me and I've waited all these years to confront you. Is he really mine?"

"Yes, George, he's yours," said Mildred, "but the other eleven aren't."

That's a terrible joke but it illustrates the diversity of offspring that can come from two fertile parents. It also raises an important question: What happens when you as a mother or father don't like the particular temperament with which your child is equipped? That is a common source of agitation among parents. Though they may never even admit their negative feelings to each other, they struggle with the fact one child is a profound disappointment to them. He is an embarrassment in public and an irritant at home. It may be his extreme shyness that galls them, or his extrovertish personality— or maybe his giddiness. Perhaps it is an athletic father with an uncoordinated son, or an overweight mother who desperately wanted, but didn't get, a thin daughter. For whatever reason, they had hoped to see the signs of greatness emerging in this child; instead, he turns out to be an intolerable misfit in the family. What then, my friends? What happens if *you* are the mother or father who dislikes one or more of your offspring?

Let's acknowledge that some children are easier to love than others. Haven't you heard it said about a particular boy or girl, "That is the sweetest kid I've ever known. I could just hug him to pieces"? We've all seen children like that who naturally attract us to them. But there are other children, millions of them, who lack that natural charm. They push people away from them, including their own families, without even understanding why.

When bonding fails to occur between parents and a particular child, both generations stand to suffer. The mother, especially, is likely to experience great feelings of guilt for her lack of affection for this individual. She recognizes his emotional needs and knows it is her responsibility to meet them, but something inside makes it difficult to respond. Instead, she reacts negatively toward this son or daughter. Ordinary childish behavior that would have been ignored in one of her other kids may bring flashes of anger toward this "problem" individual. Then she experiences more guilt for hurting someone so innocent and vulnerable. It is an emotional pit into which many parents have tumbled.

Such rejection is even more destructive from the child's point of view. Even if he can't explain it, he can feel the wall that separates him from his parents. He is especially sensitive to any preference or bias in favor of his siblings. By comparing himself with them, he gets a clearer picture of his standing in the family. If he concludes he is unloved and hated in that inner circle, his pain may manifest itself in unrestrained rebellion during the adolescent years. I've seen it happen a thousand times.

A recent guest on our Focus on the Family radio broadcast, who I'll call Susan, described her own experiences as a rejected child. Her father had returned from World War II in 1945 to discover that his wife had given birth to a baby girl who wasn't his. Susan was that infant. As the living symbol of his wife's infidelity, she was hated by her father. When she was nine years old, she found a loaded 38-caliber pistol hidden in a drawer. She was showing it to a friend when her mother burst into the room. The woman grabbed the gun from Susan and said "I hid this pistol so your dad wouldn't shoot you with it. He hates your guts and one of these days he will kill you."

For the next five years, Susan was subjected to the most terrible rejection at home. Then when she was fourteen, her mother said with intensity, "I just have to be really honest with you, Susan. You've been a problem in our marriage since the day you were born, and your dad hates you. He will never change. The best thing for you to do is to leave." Susan packed a bag and headed for California.

A person of lesser character would have been shattered by such mistreatment at home. Susan, however, managed to land on her feet. She was introduced to Jesus Christ while still a teenager, and she has devoted her life to helping others cope with their own pressures and fears.

Susan's story illustrates the intense hatred that parents can harbor for one or more of their children. When it occurs during the formative years, the despised son or daughter usually becomes twisted and crippled for the rest of his or her life. But we have been describing a more subtle and less deliberate form of rejection. It occurs in response to what might be called a parent's "private disappointment." It is not as overt as the hatred inflicted on Susan, but its pain can be almost as devastating.

Let me offer a few suggestions that may help. First, I believe it is possible in many cases to override one's emotions by an ironclad determination of the will. Feelings often follow behavior. If you make up your mind to love and care for each of your children equally, you might be surprised to find that the barriers isolating that "special" boy or girl are crumbling. What I'm saying is that human emotions are flighty and fickle. You *must* rule them with the rational mind. Do not permit yourself to be repelled from that youngster who needs and depends on you for his very sustenance. The stakes are too high!

Second, be especially wary of the game called "comparison." It's a killer! I'm convinced that most parents indulge regularly in this practice of comparing their kids with everyone else's. They want to know who is brightest, tallest, prettiest, healthiest, most mature, most athletic, and most obedient. It is fun to play as long as they win. Sooner or later, however, they're bound to lose. Their son's or daughter's greatest weakness will glow in the light of another child's strengths. It is an unsettling experience.

Our concern, of course, is for the parents whose child compares unfavorably with every other child around him. Perhaps he is mentally slow or physically handicapped or emotionally unbalanced. His parents hammer themselves with his shortcomings every day of his life. They strain to make him become what he is not . . . what he can never be. Little things gnaw at their insides. The children's program at church, for example, features the bright cutie who wows the congregation. *Just once*, they think, *would it hurt to choose our daughter? Would it violate some unwritten law of the universe to feature the least remarkable child in the starring role?* They think these thoughts, but they say nothing. No one would understand.

Have you played the comparison game? Have you thought to yourself, *If only Laurie was more like April, who is so soft and feminine. Laurie is so . . . so brash, you know? There are times when I just wish she could be—different?*

Don't do it, parents. I've lived long enough to know that circumstances may not be as they seem. April may turn out to be the problem child in the long run. Laurie may be the jewel. Either way, the worth of these kids is not dependent on the characteristics that separate them. None of us is perfect, and there is room in this world for every individual into whom an eternal soul has been breathed. My advice is to take the child God sends to you and "go with the flow." You and he will be much more contented for it!

I know this is difficult advice to follow. Parents of the shy child, for example, often ask me how they can pull him out of his shell and make him outgoing with strangers. At home he says the most profound things and shares his observations on the universe. But in public, his tongue becomes wedged to the side of his cheek. His neck curves downward and he appears deaf.

"Billy," says his exasperated father, "can't you say hello to Pastor Wilson? Billy? Billy! Has the cat got your tongue?"

The cat does *not* have Billy's tongue. It is merely stuck to his jaw, to the embarrassment of his father.

Why is Billy so introverted? Is it because he has been hurt or rejected in the past? Perhaps. But it is more likely that he was born that way, and no amount of goading by his parents will make him outgoing, flamboyant, or confident. It is a function of his temperament. Thus, I am again recommending that his parents go with the flow—accepting Billy the way God made him.

On behalf of the parent who has the greatest difficulty accepting a child the way he is, it might be helpful to ventilate those feelings with a husband, wife, or close friend. Then determine to love this unlovable boy or girl come what may. You *can* do it! There are qualities in your special youngster that may not have been seen before. Find them. Cultivate them. And then give God time to make something beautiful in his little life!

2. Grab the Reins of Authority Early

I cannot overemphasize the importance of "taking charge" of a strong-willed child during the early years of his life. This is not accomplished by being harsh, gruff, or stern. Instead, the relationship is produced by confident and steady leadership. You are the boss. You are in charge. If you believe it, the child will accept it also.

Unfortunately, many mothers are tentative and insecure in approaching their young children today. A pediatrician friend told me about a telephone call he received from the anxious mother of a six-month-old baby.

"I think he has a fever," she said nervously.

"Well," the doctor replied, "did you take his temperature?"

"No," she said, "he won't let me insert the thermometer."

I genuinely hope this woman's baby does not turn out to be a gutsy toddler bent on world dominion. He'll blow his shaky mother right out of the saddle. Like the little girl on the airplane, he will sense her insecurity and step into the power vacuum she has created.

Susannah Wesley, mother of eighteenth-century evangelists John and Charles Wesley, reportedly raised seventeen vigorous and healthy children. Toward the end of her life, John asked her to express her philosophy of mothering to him in writing. Copies of her reply are still in existence today. As you will see from the excerpts that follow, her beliefs reflect the traditional understanding of child-rearing:

> In order to form the minds of children, the first thing to be done is to conquer the will, and bring them into an obedient temper. To inform the understanding is a work of time, and must with children proceed by slow degrees as they are able to bear it; *but the subjecting of the will is a thing which must be done at once, and the sooner the better!*
>
> For by neglecting timely correction, *they will contract a stubbornness and obstinacy which is hardly ever after conquered,* and never without using such severity as would be painful to me as to the children. In the esteem of the world, those who withhold timely

correction would pass for kind and indulgent parents, whom I call cruel parents, who permit their children to get habits which they know must afterward be broken. Nay, some are so stupidly fond as in sport to teach their children to do things which in the after while, they must severely beat them for doing.

Whenever a child is corrected, it must be conquered; and this will be no hard matter to do, if it be not grown headstrong by too much indulgence. And, if the will of a child is totally subdued, and if it be brought to revere and stand in awe of the parents, then a great many childish follies and inadvertencies may be passed by. Some should be overlooked and taken no notice of, and others mildly reproved. *But no willful transgressions ought ever to be forgiven children, without chastisement, more or less as the nature and circumstances of the offense shall require.*

I cannot dismiss this subject. *As self-will is the root of all sin and misery, so whatever cherishes this in children insures their after wretchedness and faithlessness, whatever checks and mortifies, promotes their future happiness and piety.* This is still more evident if we further consider that Christianity is nothing less than doing the will of God, and not our own; that the one grand impediment to our temporal and eternal happiness being this self-will. No indulgence of it can be trivial, no denial unprofitable.

Does that sound harsh by twentieth-century standards? Perhaps. I might use different words to guard against parental oppression and overbearance. Nevertheless, in my view, Mrs. Welsey's basic understanding is correct. If the strong-willed child is allowed by indulgence to develop "habits" of defiance and disrespect during his early childhood, those characteristics will haunt him for the next twenty years. Note also that Mrs. Wesley recommended overlooking "childish follies and inadvertencies," but never to ignore "willful transgressions." What did she mean?

I attempted to distinguish between these categories of behavior in my earlier book, *Dare to Discipline*. It is interesting to see the congruity between my perspective and that of Mrs. Wesley, in spite of the two hundred years separating our times. Perhaps we drew our understandings from the same source . . . ? This is what I wrote about seventeen years ago:

> The issue of respect can be a useful tool in knowing when to punish and how excited one should get about a given behavior. First, the parent should decide whether an undesirable behavior represents a direct challenge of his authority—to his position as the father or mother. Punishment should depend on that evaluation. For example, suppose little Walter is acting silly in the living room and he falls into a table, breaking many expensive china cups and other trinkets. Or suppose he loses his bicycle or leaves Dad's best saw out in the rain. These are acts of childish irresponsibility and should be handled as such. Perhaps the parent should have the child work to pay for the losses—depending on the age and maturity of the child, of course. However, these examples do not constitute direct challenges to authority.

Thus far, I was dealing with what Mrs. Wesley called "follies and inadvertencies." Then we turned a corner.

They do not emanate from willful, haughty disobedience. In my opinion, spankings should be reserved for the moment a child (age ten or less) expresses a defiant "I will not!" or "You shut up!" When a youngster tries this kind of stiff-necked rebellion, you had better take it out of him, and pain is a marvelous purifier. When nose to nose confrontation occurs between you and your child, it is not the time to have a discussion about the virtues of obedience. It is not the occasion to send him in his room to pout. It is not appropriate to wait until poor, tired old dad comes plodding in from work, just in time to handle the conflicts of the day. You have drawn a line in the dirt, and the child has deliberately flopped his big hairy toe across it. Who is going to win? Who has the most courage? Who is in charge here? If you do not answer these questions conclusively for the child, he will precipitate other battles designed to ask them again and again. It is the ultimate paradox of childhood that a youngster wants to be controlled, but he insists that his parents earn the right to control him.[1]

The tougher the temperament of the child, the more critical it is to "shape his will" early in life. However, I must hasten to repeat the familiar disclaimers that have accompanied all my other writings on this subject. I am not recommending harshness and rigidity in child-rearing techniques! I don't believe in parental oppression, and indeed, our own children were not raised in such an atmosphere. Furthermore, I want to make it clear that corporal punishment is not to be imposed on babies.

Parents should not even shake their infants in anger.

As a child's head is being jerked back and forth his brain can strike the inside of the skull, causing concussions and even death. Frustrated and exhausted parents will sometimes do this to a colicky baby or one who has other irritating characteristics. It is tragic and it is against the law. If you fear you will inflict this or some other kind of violence on your child or if you have already hurt him, please call a local hotline (or 1-800-422-4453); you should seek immediate professional assistance. You owe it to your little one to get help before it is too late.

No. The philosophy I am recommending is not born of harshness. It is conceived in love. Corporal punishment is reserved specifically for moments of willful, deliberate, on-purpose defiance by a child who is old enough to understand what he is doing. These challenges to authority will begin at approximately fifteen months of age and should be met with loving firmness. A thump on the fingers or a single stinging slap on the upper legs will be sufficient to say, "you must listen when I tell you no." By your persistence you will establish yourself as the leader to whom the child owes obedience. At the same time, however, you must seek numerous and continual ways of telling this youngster how much you adore him. That formula of love and discipline has been tested and validated over many centuries of time, and it will work for you.

But why have we stressed the necessity of bringing a strong-willed child into subjection during the younger years? Can't it be accomplished later if necessary? Yes, it can, but as Susannah Wesley said, the cost becomes much higher even at four or five years of age. Why is that true?

Perhaps we can explain the process this way: Have you ever wondered why young children can learn to speak perfect Russian, Chinese, Spanish, Hebrew, or any other language to which they are exposed? No trace of an accent will be manifested. But twenty or more years later, most individuals will only be able to approximate the sounds made by natives of the particular region. Researchers now know why this is true. It is explained by a process known as "phoneme contraction" (or "sound dropout"). The larynx of a young child assumes a shape necessary to make the sounds he is learning to use at the time. It then solidifies or hardens in those positions, making it impossible or very difficult to make other sounds later in life. Thus, there is a brief window of opportunity when anything is possible, linguistically. It will soon be history.

A child's attitude toward parental authority is also like that. He passes through a brief window of opportunity during late infancy and toddlerhood when respect and "awe" can be instilled. But that pliability will not last long. If his early reach for power is successful, he will not willingly give it up—ever.

Before we leave this topic of early discipline, let me issue a warning about a common mistake made by parents of more than one child. Psychologist Bruce Baldwin calls it "sibling drift." By that he refers to the tendency of parents to require more of first- or secondborn children. They must earn or fight for everything they get. But as subsequent children come along, the parents begin to wear down. They are preoccupied elsewhere. We obtained definite evidence of this sibling drift from our survey of parents. With the arrival of each new child, the discipline of parents tended to loosen. Tables 10 and 11 disply this weakening of authority by compliant mothers and fathers. The pattern was not quite so pronounced among strong-willed parents, but it occurred nevertheless.

Without seeing these findings, Dr. Baldwin wrote, "The net effect is less stringent parental discipline and consequently diminished self-discipline in younger children. As a parent, you must exert constant energy to counter this trend so younger children grow up as responsible adults too."[2] We obviously agree.

Table 10—Changing Patterns of Discipline Among Compliant Fathers

% who are rather easy

% who are rather strict

% who are permissive

% who are rigid and severe

PERCENT OF CASES

First Born   Second Born   Third Born   Fourth and Subsequent

3. Raising the Compliant Child

Early discipline is not nearly so critical for the easy-going youngster. Even extremely permissive parents sometimes do no lasting harm to these happy and contented kids, because they are not looking for a fight. They are so good, in fact, that their parents are often blinded to a different set of problems which can develop right under their noses. Specifically, there are three pitfalls that must be avoided by parents of very compliant children. All of them tend to creep up from behind.

Table 11—Changing Patterns of Discipline among Compliant Mothers

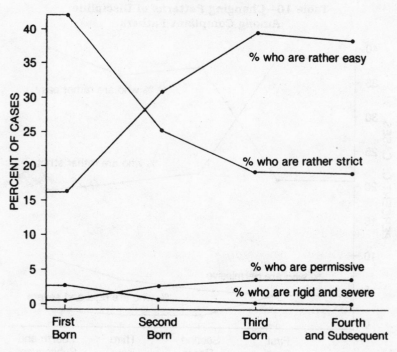

1. It is very easy to cultivate a long-term dependency relationship with the compliant individual. The bond between generations is so satisfying to the mother, especially, and so secure for the child, that neither is willing to give it up. Yet it must change in time. God did not intend for adults and their parents to have the same relationship as they did when the kids were small. Growth and maturity demand that children wriggle free from their parents' clutches and establish independent lives of their own. The compliant child has a more difficult time disengaging from the security of his nest because there has been no conflict there. By contrast, the strong-willed child is often desperate to get free. This process by which late adolescents and grown "children" are granted their independence is so important that I've devoted an entire chapter (11) to that topic.
2. The compliant child often has difficulties holding his own with his siblings.
3. The compliant child is more likely to internalize his anger and look for ways to reroute it.

These last two items deserve additional explanation because they represent a serious (but very quiet) threat to the well-being of the compliant child. My greatest concern for him is the ease with which he can be underestimated, ignored, exploited, or shortchanged at home. Haven't you seen two-child families where one youngster was a stick of dynamite who blew up regularly, and the other was an All-Star sweetheart? Under those circumstances it is not unusual for parents to take their cooperative sibling for granted. If there is an unpleasant job to be done, he will be expected to do it. Mom and Dad just don't have the energy to fight with the tiger.

If one child is to be chosen for a pleasant experience, it will probably go to the brattier of the two. He would scream bloody murder if excluded. When circumstances require one child to sacrifice or do without, you know who will be elected. Parents who favor the strong-willed child in this way are aware that they are being unfair, but their sense of justice has yielded to the pressures of practicality. They are simply too depleted and frustrated to risk irritating the tougher kid.

The consequences of such inequity should be obvious. Even though the compliant child goes along with the program and does not complain, he may accumulate a volume of resentment through the years. Isn't that what seems to have occurred to the brother of the Prodigal Son? He was the hard-working, responsible, *compliant* member of the family. Apparently, his kid brother was irresponsible, flighty, and very strong-willed. If we may be permitted to extrapolate a bit from the biblical account in Luke 15:11–32, it seems likely that there was little love lost between these sons, even before the prodigal's impulsive departure.

Disciplined elder brothers usually resent the spoiled brat who gets everything he asks for. Nevertheless, the older brother kept his thoughts to himself. He did not want to upset his father, whom he respected enormously. Then came that incredible day when little brother demanded his entire inheritance in one lump sum. The compliant son overheard the converstion and gasped in shock. *What audacity!* he thought. Then, to his amazement he heart his father grant the playboy's request. He could hear the clink of numerous gold coins being counted. Elder brother was furious. We could only assume that the departure of this sibling meant he would have to handle double chores and work longer hours in the fields. It wasn't fair that the load should fall on him. Nevertheless, he said nothing. Compliant people are inclined to hold their feelings inside.

The years passed slowly as the elder brother labored to maintain the farm. The father had grown older by then, placing a heaver strain on this firstborn son. Every day he labored from dawn to dusk in the hot sun. Occasionally, he thought about his brother living it up in the far country, and he was briefly tempted. But no. He would do what was right. Pleasing his father was the most important thing in his life.

Then, as we remember, the strong-willed goof-off ran out of money and became exceedingly hungry. He thought of his mom's cooking and the warmth of his father's fire. He clutched his rags around him and began the long journey home. When he was yet afar off, his father ran to meet him—embracing him and placing the royal robes around his shoulders. The fatted calf was killed and a great feast planned. That did it. The compliant brother could take no more. The prodigal son had secured through his folly what the elder brother could not gain through his discipline; the approval and affection of his father. His spirit was wounded!

Whether my interpretation of this parable is or is not true to the Scriptures will be left to the theologians to decide. Of this I am certain, however: strong-willed and compliant siblings have played out this drama since the days of Cain and Abel, and the responsible kid often feels like the loser. He holds his feelings inside and then pays a price for storing them. He is more susceptible as an adult to ulcers, hypertension, colitis, migraine headaches and a wide range of other illnesses. Furthermore, his sense of utter powerlessness can drive his anger underground. It may emerge in less obvious quests for control.

That introduces the significance of food as an instrument of power, which we will discuss presently. It also calls to mind the twin eating disorders of anorexia and bulimia. The anorectic individual can literally starve herself to death if not treated. She either reduces her intake of food radically or else she eats a normal meal and then promptly vomits. Sometimes she exercises compulsively while ingesting only 200–400 calories per day. Before long a 130–pound woman may weigh less than 80 pounds, and yet she may still believe herself to be overweight. The bulimic person follows the opposite pattern. She gorges uncontrollably and then "purges" herself by vomiting or the use of laxatives. Bulimia is called a "closet" disease because it often occurs in secret. It has been estimated that 20 to 30 percent of all American women of college age engage in bulimic activity! Jane Fonda has admitted to having been one of them.

Both anorexia and bulimia are thought to be minimally related to food itself. Instead, they represent a desire for *control*. The typical anorectic patient is a female in late adolescence or early adulthood. She is usually a compliant individual who was always "a good little girl." She did not play power games to any great extent. She conformed to her parents' expectations, although resenting them quietly at times. She withheld her anger and frustration at being powerless throughout the developmental years. Her father, and perhaps her mother, were strong individuals who took her submission for granted. Then one day, her need for control was manifested in a serious eating disorder. There, at least, was one area where she could be the boss.

Treatment for anorectic and bulimic individuals is a lengthy therapeutic process, and must remain the subject for another day. However, prevention of this and other common difficulties among formerly compliant children is definitely of concern to us here. I would offer these rather obvious recommendations to the parents of compliant children—especially the female of the species.

1. Treat them with respect, even when it is not demanded at gunpoint.
2. Keep them talking. Urge them to express their feelings and frustrations. Show them how to ventilate.
3. Give them their fair share in comparison to other children in the family and help them hold their own with more aggressive siblings. Remember that fences make good neighbors!
4. Grant them power commensurate with their ages. Within reason, they should make their own choices regarding clothing, hair styles, food preferences, selections of courses in school, etc. It would be quicker and more efficient to impose these decisions on the compliant individual. Resist the temptation!
5. Hold them close and then let them go. Do not continue to "parent" them after the task should be completed.
6. Keep an eye on your daughter's weight after

thirteen years of age. Seek prompt help from specialists if signs of trouble develop.

There's nothing simple about raising kids, is there? Even in the case of the "easiest" children, being a parent requires all the intelligence, tact, wisdom, and cunning we can muster. Obviously, it is no job for cowards.

4. Keep Your Sense of Humor

Laughter is the key to survival during the special stresses of the child-rearing years. If you can see the delightful side of your assignment, you can also deal with the difficult. Almost every day I hear from mothers who would agree. They use the ballast of humor to keep their boats in an upright position. They also share wonderful stories with me.

One of my favorites came from the mother of two small children. This is what she wrote.

Dear Dr. Dobson:

A few months ago, I was making several phone calls in the family room where my three-year-old daughter, Adrianne, and my five-month-old son, Nathan, were playing quietly. Nathan loves Adrianne, who has been learning how to mother him gently since the time of his birth.

I suddenly realized that the children were no longer in view. Panic-stricken, I quickly hung up the phone and went looking for the pieces. Down the hall and around the corner, I found the children playing cheerfully in Adrianne's bedroom.

Relieved and upset, I shouted, "Adrianne, you know

you are not allowed to carry Nathan! He is too little and you could hurt him if he fell!"

Startled, she answered, "I didn't, Mommy.'

Knowing he couldn't crawl, I suspiciously demanded, "Well, then, how did he get all the way into your room?"

Confident of my approval for her obedience, she said with a smile, "I rolled him!"

He is still alive and they are still best friends.

Can't you imagine how this kid felt during his journey down the hall? I'll bet the walls and ceiling are still spinning past his eyes! He didn't complain, however, so I assume he enjoyed the experience.

Another parent told me that her three-year-old daughter had recently learned that Jesus will come to live in the hearts of those who invite Him. That is a very difficult concept for a young child to assimilate, and this little girl didn't quite grasp it. Shortly thereafter she and her mother were riding in the car and the three-year-old suddenly came over and put her ear to her mother's chest.

"What are you doing?" asked the mother.

"I'm listening to Jesus in your heart," replied the child. The woman permitted the little girl to listen for a few seconds, and then she asked, "Well. What did you hear?"

The child replied, "Sounds like He's making coffee to me."

Who else but a toddler would come up with such a unique and delightful observation? If you live or work around kids, you need only listen. They will punctuate your world with mirth. They will also keep you off balance much of the time. I learned that fact several years before I became a father. As part of my professional training at the University of Southern California, I was required to teach elementary school for two years. Those were among the most informative years of my life, as I quickly learned what kids are like. It was also an initiation by fire.

Some days were more difficult than others, like the morning a kid named Thomas suddenly became ill. He lost his breakfast (thirty-seven scrambled eggs) with no warning to his fellow students or to me. I can still recall a room full of panic-stricken sixth-graders climbing over chairs and desks to escape Thomas' volcanic eruptions. They stood around the walls of the room, holding their throats and going "eeeeuuuuyuckk!" One of them was more vocal in his disgust than the others, prompting a fellow student to say, "I wouldn't talk, Norbert. You did it last year!"

It was quite a morning for a new teacher. The lunch bell saved me, and having lost my appetite, I went outside to supervise students on the playground. Since I had not grown up in California, I was interested in an apparatus called tetherball. As I stood there watching two boys competing violently with each other, a cute little sixth-grade girl named Doris came and stood beside me. Presently she asked, "Would you like to play?"

"Sure," I said. It was a mistake.

Doris was twelve years old and she was a tetherball freak! I was twenty-five years old and I couldn't get the hang of the game. The tether would change the trajectory of the ball and I kept swinging wildly at the air. My students gathered around and I became very self-conscious about my performance. There I was, 6' 2" tall and a self-proclaimed jock, yet I was getting clobbered by this little girl. Then it happened.

Doris decided to go for broke. She spiked the ball with all her might and drove it straight up my nose. I never even saw it coming. The whole world began spinning and my nose was vibrating like a tuning fork. I really thought I was going to die. My eyes were streaming tears and my ears were humming like a beehive. Yet, what could I do? Twenty kids had seen Doris ring my bell, and I couldn't let them know how badly I was hurt. So I went on playing even though I couldn't see the ball. It's a wonder Doris didn't whack me again.

Thank goodness for the afternoon bell. I took my pulsating nose back to the classroom and resolved to accept no more challenges from seventy-five-pound girls. They're dangerous.

5. The Establishment of Faith

Finally, may I urge you as parents of young children, whether compliant or strong-willed, to provide for them an unshakable faith in Jesus Christ. This is your *most* important function as mothers and fathers. How can anything else compare in significance to the goal of keeping the family circle unbroken in the life to come? What an incredible objective to work toward!

If the salvation of our children is really that vital to us, then our spiritual training should begin before children can even comprehend what it is all about. They should grow up seeing their parents on their knees before God, talking to Him. They will learn quickly at that age and will never forget what they've seen and heard. Even if they reject their faith later, the remnant of it will be with them for the rest of their lives. This is why we are instructed to ". . . bring them

up in the nurture and admonition of the Lord"
(Ephesians 6:4, KJV).

Again, I was fortunate to have had parents who understood this principle. After I was grown they told me that I
attempted to pray before I learned to talk. I watched them
talk to God and then attempted to imitate the sounds I had
heard. Two years later, at three years of age, I made a conscious decision to become a Christian. You may think it
impossible at such an age, but it happened. I remember the
occasion clearly today. I was attending a Sunday evening
church service and was sitting near the back with my
mother. My father was the pastor, and he invited those who
wished to do so to come pray at the altar. Fifteen or twenty
people went forward, and I joined them spontaneously. I
recall crying and asking Jesus to forgive my sins. I know
that sounds strange, but that's the way it occurred. It is
overwhelming for me to think about that event today.
Imagine the King of the universe, Creator of all heaven and
earth, caring about an insignificant kid barely out of
toddlerhood! It makes no sense, but I know it happened.

Not every child will respond that early or dramatically,
of course, nor should they. Some are more sensitive to
spiritual matters than others, and they must be allowed
to progress at their own pace. But in no sense should we
as their parents be casual or neutral about their training. Their world should sparkle with references to Jesus
and to our faith. That is the meaning of Deuteronomy
6:6–9, "These commandments that I give you today are
to be upon your hearts. Impress them on your children.
Talk about them when you sit at home and when you
walk along the road, when you lie down and when you
get up. Tie them as symbols on your hands and bind

them on your foreheads. Write them on the doorframes of your houses and on your gates."

I believe this commandment from the Lord is one of the most crucial verses for parents in the entire Bible. It instructs us to surround our children with godly teaching. References to spiritual things are not to be reserved just for Sunday morning or even for a bedtime prayer. They should permeate our conversation and the fabric of our lives. Why? Because our children are watching our every move during those early years. They want to know what is most important to us. If we hope to instill within them a faith that will last for a lifetime, then they must see and feel our passion for God.

As a corollary to that principle, I must remind you that children miss nothing in sizing up their parents. If you are only half-convinced of your beliefs, they will quickly discern that fact. Any ethical weak spot—any indecision on your part—will be incorporated and then magnified in your sons and daughters. Like it or not, we are on the hook. Their faith or their faithlessness will be a reflection of our own. As I've said, our children will eventually make their own choices and set the course of their lives, but those decisions will be influenced by the foundations we have laid. Someone said, "The footsteps a boy follows are the ones his father thought he covered up." It is true.

That brings me to another extremely important point, even though it is controversial. I firmly believe in acquainting children with God's judgment and wrath while they are young. Nowhere in the Bible are we instructed to skip over the unpleasant scriptures in our teaching. The wages of sin is death, and children have a right to understand that fact.

I remember my mother reading the story of Samson to me when I was about nine years old. After this mighty warrior fell into sin, you will recall, the Philistines put out his eyes and held him as a common slave. Some time later, Samson repented before God and he was forgiven. He was even given back his awesome strength. But my mother pointed out that he never regained his eyesight nor did he ever live in freedom again. He and his enemies died together as the temple collapsed upon them.

"There are terrible consequences to sin," she told me solemnly. "Even if you repent and are forgiven, you will still suffer for breaking the laws of God. They are there to protect you. If you defy them, you will pay the price for your disobedience."

Then she talked to me about gravity, one of God's physical laws. "If you jump from a ten-story building, you can be certain that you will crash when you hit the ground. It is inevitable. You must also know that God's *moral* laws are just as real as his physical laws. You can't break them without crashing sooner or later."

Finally, she taught me about heaven and hell and the great Judgment Day when those who have been covered by the blood of Jesus will be separated eternally from those who have not. It made a profound impression on me.

Many parents would not agree with my mother's decision to acquaint me with the nature of sin and its consequences. They have said to me, "Oh, I wouldn't want to paint such a negative picture for my kids. I want them to think of God as a loving Father, not as a wrathful judge who punishes us." In so doing, they withhold a portion of the truth from their children. He is both a God of love and a God of judgment. There are 116 places in the Bible where we are told to "fear the Lord." By what authority do we eliminate these references in describing who God is to our children?

I am thankful that my parents and my church had the courage to acquaint me with the "warning note" in Scripture. It was this awareness of sin and its consequences that kept me moral at times when I could have fallen into sexual sin. Biblical faith was a governor—a checkpoint beyond which I was unwilling to go. By that time I was not afraid of my parents. I could have fooled them. But I could not get away from the all-seeing eye of the Lord. I knew I would stand accountable before Him someday, and that fact gave me the extra motivation to make responsible decisions.

I can't overstate the importance of teaching divine accountability to your strong-willed children, especially. Since their tendency is to test the limits and break the rules, they will need this internal standard to guide their behavior. Not all will listen to it, but some will. But while doing that, be careful to *balance* the themes of love and justice as you teach your children about God. To tip the scales in either direction is to distort the truth and create confusion in a realm where understanding is of utmost significance.

---

[1] *Dare to Discipline* (Wheaton, Ill: Tyndale House Publishers, 1970), 27–28.

[2] Bruce A. Baldwin, "Growing Up Responsible, (Part 2), Parental Problems with Discipline Procedures," *Piedmont Airline* (December 1985):11.

Chapter Seven

Power Games

*I*n our efforts to understand the strong-willed child, we must ask ourselves why he or she is so fond of conflict. If given the opportunity to choose between war and peace, most of us would prefer tranquility. Yet the toughminded kid goes through life like a runaway lawn mower. He'll chew up anything that gets in his way. The taller the grass, the better he survives and thrives. What makes him like that? What drives him to challenge his mother and defy his father? They are not his enemies. Why would he resist their loving leadership from the earliest days of childhood? Why does he seem to enjoy irritating his siblings and goading his neighbors? Why does he throw erasers when his teachers turn their backs, and why won't he do his homework? Indeed, why can't he be like his compliant brothers and sisters?

These are interesting questions that I have pondered for years. Now I believe I'm beginning to understand some of the motivating forces that drive the strong-willed kid to attack his world. Deep within his or her spirit is a raw desire for *power*. We can define power in this context as control—control of others, control of our circumstances and, especially, control of ourselves. The strong-willed child is not the only one who seeks power, of course. He differs from the rest of the human family only in degree, not in kind. We all want to be the boss and that desire is evident in very young children. Remember the toddler who rode his tricycle into the street and shouted angrily at his mother? The real issue between them was a matter of power and who would hold it. We see the same struggle when an adolescent slams doors and flees in his car, or when a husband and wife fight over finances, or when an elderly woman refuses to move to a nursing home. The common thread is the desire to run our own lives—and that of everyone else if given the chance. We vary in intensity of this impulse, as we will see, but it seems to motivate all of us to one degree or another.

The desire for control appears to have its roots in the very early hours after birth. Studies of newborns indicate that they typically "reach" for the adults around them on the first or second day of life. By that I mean they behave in ways designed to entice their guardians to meet their needs. Some will perfect the technique in the years that follow.

Even mature adults who ought to know better are usually involved in power games with other people. It happens whenever human interests collide, but it is especially prevalent in families. Husbands, wives, children, siblings, in-laws, and parents all have reason to manipulate each other. It is fascinating to sit back and watch them push, pull, and twist. In fact, I've identified sixteen techniques that are used to obtain power in another person's life. Perhaps you will think of additional approaches as you read the list that follows:

1. *Emotional Blackmail*: "Do what I want or I'll get very angry and go all to pieces."

2. *The Guilt Trip*: "How could you do this to me after I've done so much for you?"

3. *Divine Revelation*: "God told me you should do what I want."

4. *The Foreclosure*: "Do what I want or I won't pay the bills."

5. *The Bribe*: "Do what I want and I'll make it worth your time."

6. *By Might and by Power*: "Shut up and do what I tell you!"

7. *The Humiliation*: "Do what I want or I'll embarrass you at home and abroad."

8. *The Eternal Illness*: "Don't upset me. Can't you see I'm sick?"

9. *Help from Beyond the Grave*: "Your dear father (or mother) would have agreed with me."

10. *The Adulterous Threat*: "Do what I want or I'll find someone who will."

11. *The In-law Ploy*: "Do what I want and I'll be nice to your sweet mother."

12. *The Seduction*: "I'll make you an offer you can't afford to refuse," or as Mae West said to Cary Grant, "Why doncha come up and see me some time?" She also said she used to be Snow White but she drifted.

Special approaches used by adolescents:

13. *Teenage Terror:* "Leave me alone or I'll pull a stupid adolescent stunt" (suicide, drugs, booze, wrecking the car, or hitchhiking to San Francisco).

14. *The Flunkout:* "Let me do what I want or I'll get myself booted out of Woodrow Wilson Junior High School."

15. *Fertile Follies:* "Do what I want or I'll present you with a baby!" (This threat short-circuits every nerve in a parent's body.)

16. *The Tranquilizer:* "Do what I want and I won't further complicate your stressful life."

Manipulation! It's a game any number can play, right in the privacy of your own home. The objective is to obtain power over the other players, as we have seen. It will come as no surprise to parents, I'm sure, that children can be quite gifted at power games. That is why it is important for mothers and fathers to consider this characteristic as they attempt to interpret childish behavior. Another level of motivation lies below the surface issues that seemingly cause conflicts between generations. For example, when a three-year-old runs away in a supermarket, or when a nine-year-old refuses to straighten his room, or when a twelve-year-old continues to bully his little brother, or when a sixteen-year-old smokes cigarettes or drinks liquor, they are making individual statements about power. Their rebellious behavior usually represents more than a desire to do what is forbidden. Rather, it is an expression of independence and self-assertion. It is also a rejection of adult authority, and therein lies the significance for us.

Power games begin in earnest when children are between twelve and fifteen months of age. Some get started even earlier. If you've ever watched a very young child continue to reach for an electric plug or television knob while his mother shouts, "No!", you've seen an early power game in progress. It is probably not a conscious process at this stage, but later it will be. I'm convinced that a strong-willed child of three or older is inclined to challenge his mom and dad whenever he believes he can win. He will carefully choose the weapons and select the turf on which the contest will be staged. I've called these arenas "the battlefields of childhood." Let's look at some of the Gettysburgs, Stalingrads, or Waterloos that have gone down in family history.

Bedtime

One of the earliest contests begins at eighteen months and one day of age, give or take a few hours. At precisely that time, a toddler who has gone to bed without complaining since he was born will suddenly say, "I'm not getting back in that crib again for as long as I live." That is the opening salvo in what may be a five-year battle. It happens so quickly and unexpectedly that parents may be fooled by it. They will check for teething problems, a low-grade fever, or some other discomfort. "Why *now*?" they ask. I don't know. It just suddenly occurs to toddlers that they don't want to go to bed anymore, and they will fight it tooth and nail.

Although the tactics change a bit, bedtime will continue to be a battlefield for years to come. Any creative six-year-old can delay going to bed for at least forty-five minutes by an energetic and well-conceived system of stalling devices. By the time his mother gets his pajamas on, brings him six glasses of water, takes him to the bathroom twice, helps him say his prayers, and then scolds him for wandering out of his bedroom a time or two, she is thoroughly exhausted. It happens night after night.

A college friend of mine named Jim found himself going through this bedtime exercise every evening with his five-year-old son, Paulie. Jim recognized the tactics as a game and decided he didn't want to play anymore. He sat down with his son that evening and said, "Now, Paulie, things are going to be different tonight. I'm going to get you dressed for bed; you can have a drink of water and then we'll pray together. When that is done I'm walking out the door and I don't intend to come back. Don't call me again. I don't want to hear a peep from you until morning. Do you understand?"

Paulie said, "Yes, Daddy."

When the chores were completed, final hugs were exchanged and the lights were turned out. Jim told his son good night and left the room. Sweet silence prevailed in the house. But not for long. In about five minutes, Paulie called his father and asked for another drink of water.

"No way, Paulie," said his dad. "Don't you remember what I said? Now go to sleep."

After several minutes, Paulie appealed again for a glass of water. Jim was more irritated this time. He spoke sharply and advised his son to forget it. But the boy would not be put off. He waited for a few minutes and then reopened the case. Every time Paulie called his dad, Jim became more irritated. Finally, he said, "If you ask for water one more time I'm going to come in there and spank you!"

That quieted the boy for about five minutes and then he said, "Daddy, when you come in here to spank me would you bring me a glass of water please?"

The kid got the water. He did not get the spanking.

One of the ways of enticing children (perhaps age four to eight) to go to bed is by the use of fantasy. For example, I told my son and daughter about "Mrs. White's Party" when they were little. Mrs. White was an imaginary lady who threw the most fantastic celebrations in the middle of the night. She ran an amusement park that made Disneyland boring by comparison. Whatever was of interest to the children was worked into her repertoire— dogs, cats, sweets of all varieties, water slides, cartoons, thrilling rides, and anything else that excited Danae's and Ryan's imaginations. Of course, the *only* way they could go to Mrs. White's Party was to be asleep. No one who was awake would ever get an invitation. It was fun to watch our son and daughter jump into bed and concentrate to go to sleep. Though it never happened, I wish I could have generated such interest that they would have actually dreamed about Mrs. White. Usually, the matter was forgotten the next morning.

By hook or crook, fantasy or reality, you must win the great bedtime battle. The health of your child (and maybe your own) is at stake.

Food

The dinner table is another major battlefield of childhood, but it should be avoided. I have strongly advised parents not to get suckered into this arena. It is an ambush. A general always wants to engage the other army in a place where he can win, and mealtime is a lost cause. A mother who puts four green beans on a fork and resolves to sit there until the child eats them is in a powerless position. The child can outlast her. And because meals come around three times a day, he will eventually prevail.

Instead of begging, pleading, bribing, and threatening a child, I recommend that good foods be placed before him cheerfully. If he chooses not to eat, then smile and send him on his way. He'll be back. When he returns, take the same food out of the refrigerator, heat it and set it before him again. Sooner or later, he will get hungry enough to eat. Do not permit snacking or substituting sweets for nutritious foods. But also do not fear the physical effects of hunger. A child will not starve in the presence of good things to eat. There is a gnawing feeling inside that changes one's attitude from "Yuck!" to "Yum!", usually within a few hours.

We have already talked about anorexia and bulimia, eating disorders related to parental power. Obviously, food can be the focal point of great struggles between generations.

Schoolwork

Perhaps there is *no* greater source of conflict between generations today than schoolwork, and especially that portion assigned to be done at home. This is another battle-field where all the advantages fall to the youngster. Only he knows for sure what was assigned and how the work is supposed to be done. The difficult child will capitalize on this information gap between home and school, claiming that "I got it all done in school," or "I have nothing to do tonight." He reminds me of the kid who brought home 4 Fs and a C on his report card. When his dad asked what he thought the problem was, he said, "I guess I've been concentrating too hard on one subject."

Parents should know that *most* students go through an academic valley sometime between the sixth and ninth grades in school. Some will quit working altogether during this time. Others will merely decrease their output. Very few will remain completely unaffected. The reason is the massive assault made on adolescent senses by the growing-up process. Self-confidence is shaken to its foundation. Happy hormones crank into action and sex takes over center stage. Who can think about school with all that going on? Or better yet, who wants to? As parents, you should watch for this diversion and not be dismayed when it comes. We'll discuss the underachiever later in this book.

Vacations and Special Days

Tell me why it is that children are the most obnoxious and irritating on vacations and during other times when we are specifically trying to please them? By all that is fair and just, you would expect them to think, *Boy! Mom and Dad are really doing something nice for us. They are taking us on this expensive vacation when they could have spent the money on themselves. And Dad would probably have preferred to go fishing (that's true) or something else he wanted to do. But they care about us and have included us in their plans. Wow! I'm going to be as nice and cooperative as possible. I'll try to get along with my sister and I won't make any unusual demands. What a fun trip this will be!*

Do kids think that way? Fat chance! There is no such thing as intergenerational gratitude.

Before the family has even left town, the troops are fighting over who gets to sit by the window and which one will hold the dog. Little Sister yells, "I'm telling!" every few minutes. Tensions are also building in the front seat. By the time they get to Phoenix, Dad is ready to blow his cork. It was tough enough for him to complete his office work and pack the car. But this bickering is about to drive him crazy. For four hundred miles, he has endured arguments, taunts, jabs, pinches, tears, tattling, and unscheduled bathroom breaks. Now he's starting to lose control. Twice he swings wildly at writhing bodies in the backseat. He misses and hurts his shoulder. He's driving faster by this time but he's quit talking. The only clues to what he's feeling are his bloodshot eyes and the occasional twitch in his left cheek. Happy vacation, Pop. You have thirteen days to go.

Recently I received a letter from a mother who had just returned from a stressful vacation similar to the one I described. For days, their two sons had whined and complained, insulting and fighting with each other. They kicked the back of their father's seat for hours at a time. Finally, his fuse burned down to the dry powder. He pulled the car over to the side of the road and jerked the boys outside. Judgment Day had arrived. After spanking them both, he shoved them back into the car and warned them to keep their mouths shut. "If I hear a peep from either of you for thirty minutes," he warned, "I'll give you some more of what you just had!" The boys got the message. They remained mute for thirty minutes, after which the older lad said, "Is it all right to talk now?"

The father said sternly, "Yes. What do you want to say?"

"Well," continued the boy, "when you spanked us back there my shoe fell off. We left it in the road."

It was the only good pair of shoes the kid owned. This time Mom went berserk and flailed at the backseat like a crazy lady. So ended another great day of family togetherness.

Is this the way parents should deal with a period of irritation from their children? Of course not, but let's face it. Parents are people. They have their vulnerabilities and flash points too. The children should have been separated or perhaps offered spankings much earlier in the journey. It is when parents are desperately trying to avoid punishment that their level of irritation reaches a dangerous level. By then, anything can happen. That is why I have contended that those who oppose corporal punishment on the grounds that it leads to child abuse are wrong. By stripping parents of the ability to handle frustrating behavior at an early stage, they actually increase the possibility that harm will be done to children as tempers rise.

Before we leave the matter of family vacations, let's deal with why it is that children seem to become more obnoxious on those special days. There are two good reasons for it. First, adults and children alike tend to get on each other's nerves when they are cooped up together for extended periods of time. But also, a difficult child apparently feels compelled to reexamine the boundaries whenever he thinks they may have moved. This was certainly true of our children. On days when we planned trips to Disneyland, ski trips, or other holidays, we could count on them to become testy. It was as though they were obligated to ask, "Since this is a special day, what are the rules now?" We would sometimes have to punish or scold them during times when we were specifically trying to build relationships. Your strong-willed kids may do the same. Perhaps that's why Erma Bombeck said, "The family that plays together gets on one another's nerves."

Other battlefields of early childhood include clothing and hair styles, doing the dishes and household chores, demands for candy and treats in supermarkets, getting up in time to catch the school bus, taking regular baths, talking sassy to mom and keeping the child's room clean. (One mother told me her ten-year-old's bedroom was such a mess that she would have to get a tetanus shot to walk through it.) The number of these routine skirmishes between parents and children is virtually endless. A child can use almost any pretext to launch a new crusade—or had you already noticed?

To repeat our thesis, these trouble spots between generations are not simply matters of differing opinion. If the conflicts amounted to no more than that, then negotiation and compromise would resolve them very quickly. Instead, they represent staging areas where the authority of the parent can be challenged and undermined. The question being asked is not so much, "Can I have my way?" as it is, "Who's in charge here?" (Remember, now, that I'm describing the motivation of very strong-willed children. The compliant child is more subtle in his maneuvers for power.)

With the passage of time, the battles do tend to become more intense. What began as relatively minor struggles over bedtime or homework can develop into the most terrible conflicts. Some teenagers put their parents through hell on earth. Deep, searing wounds are inflicted that may never fully heal. For now, however, I want to conclude this discussion by explaining the great significance of power and its ramifications for parents. Everything said to this point is merely prologue to the message in paragraphs that follow. Please give special emphasis to this remaining section as you read.

The sense of power that is so attractive to children and to the rest of humanity is actually a very dangerous thing. Men have deceived, exploited, and killed to get it. Those who have achieved it have often been destroyed in its grasp. Lord Acton said, "Power corrupts, and absolute power corrupts absolutely." History has proved him right.

The most bloodthirsty men who ever lived were driven by an insatiable lust for power. In the effort to dominate the world, Adolph Hitler set off a conflagration that claimed fifty million lives. Joseph Stalin is said to have murdered twenty to thirty million people during his reign of terror. On one occasion, Stalin reportedly sent his secret police to the little town where he was raised with orders to kill the teachers who had instructed him as a child. Imagine the brutality! Apparently, he wanted to leave no witnesses to his mediocre beginnings. This is where the lust for power leads when it is unbridled.

Our concern, however, is not limited to the behavior of dictators and despots. Power has a negative effect wherever it comes to rest. I've known many famous physicians and surgeons, for example, who exercised vast authority in the medical community. Patients worshiped them; nurses feared them; colleagues respected them; and friends envied them. They seemed to have it all. But how did this adulation affect their personalities? Did they grow more humble and self-effacing as their ego needs were met? Hardly! They tended to become more infantile in their demands, or they became tyrannical and sought to crush anyone who got in their way.

Notorious physicians are not the only ones who have trouble handling power. The same is true of successful actors, musicians, ministers, lawyers, and military generals in times of war. Study the historical profiles of great military generals like George Patton or Douglas MacArthur. Most were proud and arrogant men. A story is told about the haughty British general, Bernard Montgomery, who was giving a speech near the end of his life. He said, "You will remember when God said to Moses there in the wilderness—and I think rightly so—" Who but a commander of armies would dare critique the words of the Lord Himself?

United States presidents have also been known to take themselves too seriously, and Lyndon Johnson was among the worst. During his years in the White House, he was a power monger, terrorizing his aides for their minor mistakes and oversights. I'm told, for example, that he became furious when they forgot to restock the presidential airplane with root beer, his favorite soft drink. "No rut beer!?" he would scream in his Texas drawl. "Whaddaya mean no rut beer?!" He couldn't believe anyone would have the audacity to ignore his whims in this way.

It is interesting that five United States presidents in the twentieth century have won landslide electoral victories and achieved the power to which they were entitled.

Predictably, perhaps, all five experienced their greatest crises shortly thereafter. Harding and the Teapot Dome Scandal; Roosevelt and the Supreme Court debacle; Johnson and the Vietnam war; Nixon and the Watergate affair; and Reagan and the Iran-Contra connection. Time after time, history illuminates the destructive nature of raw power. Proverbs 27:21 states, ". . . man is tested by the praise he receives."

Chuck Colson lived through the Watergate debacle that brought down President Richard Nixon. As a senior member of the White House staff during an era when presidential influence was maximal, Colson knew how to use power. He was also quite willing to abuse it. He worked just a few feet from the Oval Office and his orders carried the authority of the president himself. By simply making a phone call, he could send a detachment of troops anywhere in the world. He could have the presidential helicopter land on the White House lawn within minutes to take him where he wished to go. He conferred with the Soviets and with our allies on matters of monumental importance. Yes, Chuck Colson experienced the meaning of political power in all its glory, and his fall from that lofty perch was one of the most dramatic descents in American history.

After his conviction in the Watergate scandal, Colson was sentenced to serve two years in the federal penitentiary at Maxwell Prison Camp in Florida. Upon arrival, this proud governmental leader was systematically shorn of his dignity. He was stripped, searched, and dusted for lice. He was placed in an eight-foot cell with a stinking open toilet. A guard came by every two hours and shined a flashlight in his eyes. Colson, who had conferred with prime ministers, emperors, and princes, now lived and worked with rapists, murderers, thieves, and child molesters. He was utterly powerless for some seven months.

How impressive it is that Chuck Colson chose not to reconstruct his power base when he was released from prison. He could have gone back to his law practice in New York, with its six-figure income, a yacht and the other trappings of opulence. Instead, he founded Prison Fellowship Ministries to assist the down-and-outers of the world. Why would a man deny himself in that way?

Because he found a "higher power" in a personal relationship with Jesus Christ. It totally revolutionized his life. I admire this man greatly and am honored to call him my friend.

If you talk to Chuck Colson today, he will warn you of the dangers of power. He should know. He was nearly destroyed by it. He will also tell you how he manipulated naive Christians when he was in the White House. He dazzled them with presidential power and molded them to his political purposes. Finally, he will remind you that Jesus came without power and consistently resisted His disciples' desire for it. Jesus taught them, ". . . he who is least among you all—he is the greatest" (Luke 9:48).

Perhaps you have foreseen how this discussion of presidential politics and professional pride is related to the discipline of children, but let me lay it out. If power can be destructive to mature adults who think they know how to handle it, imagine what it will do to a mere child. Think again of the three-year-old boy on the tricycle, described in the second chapter. He had already achieved virtual independence from his mother. There he was, fresh out of *babyhood,* yet he had become his own boss. That's pretty heady stuff for a kid who's only three feet high. How would he choose to use all that power? Well, for starters he insisted on riding his tricycle down a busy boulevard. He is fortunate that his first taste of freedom didn't put him under the wheels of a four-thousand-pound automobile. There will be other risks in future years, of course.

One of the characteristics of those who acquire power very early is a prevailing attitude of disrespect for authority. It extends to teachers, ministers, policemen, judges, and even to God Himself. Such an individual has never yielded to parental leadership at home. Why should he submit himself to anyone else? For a rebellious teenager it is only a short step from there to drug abuse, sexual experimentation, running away, and so on. The early acquisition of power has claimed countless young victims by this very process.

What do we recommend then? Should parents retain every vestige of power for as long as possible) No! Even with its risks, self-determination is a basic human right, and we must grant it systematically to our children. To withhold that liberty too long is to incite wars of revolution. My good friend, Jay Kesler, observed that Mother England made that specific mistake with her children in the American colonies. They grew to become rebellious "teenagers" who demanded their freedom. Still she refused to release them and unnecessary bloodshed ensued. Fortunately, England learned a valuable lesson from that painful experience. Some 171 years later, she granted a peaceful and orderly transfer of power to another tempestuous offspring named India. Revolution was averted.

This, then, is our goal as parents: We must not transfer power too early, even if our children take us daily to the battlefield. Mothers who make that mistake are some of the most frustrated people on the face of the earth. On the other hand, we must not retain parental power too long, either. Control will be torn from our grasp if we refuse to surrender it voluntarily. The granting of self-determination should be matched stride for stride with the arrival of maturity, culminating with complete release during early adulthood.

Sounds easy, doesn't it? We all know better. I consider this orderly transfer of power to be one of the most delicate and difficult responsibilities in the entire realm of parenthood. We'll talk more about the "how to" in subsequent chapters.

Chapter Eight

Too Pooped to Parent

*W*e want to deal now with the problem of parental exhaustion and its effect on mothers and fathers of young children. Chronic fatigue has become an everyday occurrence for the majority of parents in North America, and its implications are difficult to overestimate. Without question, the best book I have read on this subject is entitled *Parent Burnout*, by Dr. Joseph Procaccini and Mark Kiefaber.[1] The authors describe how parents manage to squander their resources and ultimately fail in the task they care about most: raising healthy and responsible children. If you have staggered under the pressures of parenthood, I hope you will buy and read that book. In the meantime, let me provide a broad outline of its central message and add a few thoughts of my own.

Not surprisingly, perhaps, the most likely candidates for early exhaustion are the parents who are radically committed to their children. After all, if there is no "fire" there can be no burnout. These zealous and dedicated mothers and fathers are determined to provide every advantage and opportunity for the next generation from the earliest days of infancy. That is where their hearts lie. That is what they care about most. Their devotion leads them to make what they consider to be small sacrifices on behalf of the children. They often discontinue all recreational, romantic, and restful activities that would take them away from home. Even long-term friends with whom they used to associate are now given lame excuses or are ignored altogether.

Compulsive Parenting

Everything focuses on the children. They are often unwilling to leave the kids with a baby-sitter for more than a few moments. Not even Mother Teresa would qualify as guardian for an evening. They would simply never forgive themselves if something went wrong while they were frivolously indulging in fun or entertainment. Imagine how they would feel if the announcer said over the public address system, "May I have your attention? Would Mr. or Mrs. James Johnson come to a house telephone, please? Your baby-sitter needs to know where the fire extinguisher is." No way! It's not worth it. They choose to stay home.

Sometimes this exclusivity with the baby even extends to grandparents, who are enormously insulted by the situation. They have accumulated twenty-five years of parenting experience and yet they are not trusted with the grandkids for a single evening. White-hot anger flows between generations and may be remembered for the rest of their lives. Nevertheless, the parents dig in and isolate themselves further.

In other cases, grandparents are simply not available to help shoulder the load. They may live a thousand miles away and come to visit only once or twice a year. But let's be honest. Other grandmas don't want to be bothered. They're busily chasing careers of their own. The following poem, shared with me by Florence Turnridge, delightfully makes that case.

WHERE HAVE ALL THE GRANDMAS GONE?

In the dim and distant past,
  When life's tempo wasn't fast,
Grandma used to rock and knit,
  Crochet, tat and baby-sit.
When the kids were in a jam,
  They could always call on "Gram."
In that day of gracious living,
  Grandma was the gal for giving.

BUT today she's in the gym,
  Exercising to keep slim,
She's off touring with the bunch,
  Or taking clients out to lunch.
Going north to ski or curl,
  All her days are in a whirl.
Nothing seems to stop or block her,
  Now that Grandma's off her rocker!!!

Author Unknown[2]

If she's not careful, Grandma will also burn herself out and be back in her rocker again. Either way, she may not be able to offer the support to her children that grandparents provided in centuries past. The extended family is gone, leaving a young mother isolated and alone. She may pass two or four or even ten years without a significant break from the tasks of child-rearing. She feels it is a minor sacrifice to make for so great a purpose. And yet, her perspective on life is distorted. The routine events of her world are interpreted in terms of this one dimensional value system. Anything that might have the remotest negative influence on her kids becomes deeply disturbing to her, leading to overreaction and conflict. Insignificant childhood squabbles in the neighborhood, for example, or idle comments from church members can bring surprisingly heated responses. And Lord help the teacher or Sunday school worker who fails to deliver!

Compulsive parenting can also be destructive to a marriage, especially when only one parent is so inclined. If it is the mother, she may give herself totally to the children and have nothing left for her husband. He believes she has gone a little wacky with this mothering thing, and may even resent the kids for taking her away from him. She, in turn, despises his selfishness and becomes sole defender and caregiver for their children. A wedge is thereby driven between them that may someday destroy the family.

Superparenting

Please understand that I am not critical of the motives behind what might be called "superparenting." Children *are* worth our very best efforts to raise them properly, and I have spent twenty years urging parents to give them their due. Nevertheless, even a noble and necessary task can be taken to such extremes that it becomes harmful

to both the giver and the receiver. In the child's case, there is a direct link between superparenting and over-protection, an egocentric perspective on life, and in some cases, a prolonged dependency relationship with parents. In the adult context, obsessive child-rearing can lead inexorably to the condition known as parental burnout.

Procaccini and Kiefaber have provided an insightful explanation of how burnout occurs in the compulsive parent, or for that matter, in anyone who fails to take care of himself. Their concept is based on five key premises, as follows: (1) human energy is a precious resource that makes possible everything we wish to do; (2) energy is a *finite* quantity—there is a limited supply available to each of us; (3) *whenever the expenditure of energy exceeds the supply, burnout begins;* (4) parents who hope to accomplish the goals they have set for themselves and their children must not squander their vital resources foolishly; and (5) wasteful drains on that supply should be identified and eliminated, and priority given to rebuilding the reserve.

From this explanation it is understandable why burnout is an occupational hazard for parents who reserve nothing for themselves. It should also be clear why superparenting is a natural trap for those of us who share the Christian faith. Deeply ingrained within us is a philosophy that lends itself to compulsive child-rearing. The family ranks near the top of our value system, and our way of life focuses on self-sacrifice and commitment to others. Does it not seem reasonable, therefore, that we would pour every resource into this awesome task? That is our God-given assignment, isn't it?

Well, of course, it is, but I would point out that the

apostle Paul advocates moderation in *all* things (Philippians 4:5). Remember, too, that Jesus took time to rest and care for His body. On one occasion, He got in a boat and rowed away from the multitudes of sick and needy people on the shore. He could have remained there and healed thousands more, but He had apparently reached the limits of His strength. Parents *must* learn to monitor their own bodies, too, and conserve their energy for the long haul. That is, after all, in the very best interest of their children.

Lest we be misunderstood, extremely dedicated mothers and fathers are not the only parents who are inclined to overextend their resources. The routine experiences of living in today's stressful environment are sufficient in themselves to wear us out. Urgent demands are made simultaneously by our jobs, our churches, our children's schools, our friends and our civic responsibilities. The great movement of women into the labor force has left millions of mothers on the brink of nervous collapse as they attempt to combine full-time employment with full-time responsibilities at home. In her book, *Having It All*, Helen Gurley Brown advised women that it is possible to achieve multiple competing goals. She is wrong, except in rare cases. Something has to give. Again, when the demand for energy exceeds the supply, *for whatever reason*, burnout is inevitable. And children are almost always the losers in the competition for that limited resource.

But what is it like to experience parental burnout? According to Procaccini and Kiefaber, it occurs in five progressive stages, each more stressful than the ones before. The first can be called the "Gung-Ho" stage,

which has been described in preceding paragraphs. It may actually begin with the discovery of pregnancy and continue for several years. Very subtly, then, parents can move from the first to the second stage of burnout, which is characterized by persistent doubts. They know something is definitely wrong at this point, but may fail to realize how rapidly they are losing altitude. They are frequently irritated by the children and find themselves screaming on occasions. Quite often they feel drained and fatigued. A full range of psychosomatic symptoms may come and go, including back and neck aches, upset stomach, ulcers and colitis, hypertension, headaches, diarrhea, and constipation. Still, the individual may wonder, *Why do I feel this way?* Not long ago I received a classic letter from a father in the second stage of parental burnout. This is what he wrote (emphasis mine):

> The reason I'm writing is that the Lord has blessed us so much, and I should be full of joy. But I have been depressed for about 10 months now.
>
> I don't know whether to turn to a pastor, a physician, a psychologist, a nutritionist, or a chiropractor.
>
> Last September the Lord blessed us with a beautiful baby boy. He is just wonderful. He is cute and smart and strong. We just can't help but love him. *But he has been very demanding.* The thing that made it hardest for me was last semester Margie was taking classes three nights a week to finish her BA degree and I took care of little Danny. He cried and sobbed the whole time we were together. He would eventually go to sleep if I would hold him, but then I was afraid to put him down

for fear he would wake up. I was used to being able to pay my bills, work out the budget, read, file mail, answer letters, type lists, etc., in the evening, but all this had to be postponed until Margie was here.

It was a real depressing time for me. I just couldn't handle all that crying. It was worse because Margie was breast-feeding him. I got very tired and started having a great deal of trouble getting up in the morning to go to work. I started getting sick very easily.

I have not been able to cope with these things. I really should be at work at 8:00, but I haven't been there before 9:00 or 9:30 in months. *It seems like I'm always fighting the flu.* I love our baby a lot and I wouldn't trade him for anything in the world. But I don't understand why I'm so depressed. Sure, Margie gets tired because we can't seem to get Danny to bed before 11 or 12 midnight and he wakes up twice per night to be fed. But she's not depressed. *All this getting awakened at night really gets to me* and I don't even have to get up to feed him.

Another thing that has been a constant struggle is leaving Danny in the nursery at church. He isn't content to be away from us very long so they end up having to track Margie down almost every Sunday. *We hardly ever get to be together.* This has been going on for 11 months now.

There are a couple of other things that probably contribute to my depression. They are (1) responsibilities at work; we're short-handed and I'm trying to do too much; (2) spending too many weekends with yard work or trying to fix up our fixer-upper house; and (3) our finances, which are very limited. Sixty-four percent of our income goes to pay for our house and there's not much left over. We don't want Margie to go to work, so we are on a meticulous budget. It's down to the bare essentials, now. I get so tired of that.

We have all the things we would ever dream of at our age (27). Our own neat little house in a good neighborhood, a job I consider a ministry. We have a fine healthy boy, each other, and not least of all, our life in Christ.

I have no reason to be depressed and tired all the time. I come home from work so exhausted that I don't even want Danny near me. He hangs on to Margie and she can't even fix dinner if I don't get him out of her hair. I just don't know how she stands it.

She must have a higher tolerance as far as not getting anything done is concerned.

If you have any insights as to what I should do, please let me know. Thanks and God bless you.

Jack

This twenty-seven-year-old father is well on the way toward burning out. The surprising thing is that Jack is bewildered by it. When one looks at his impossible schedule, it is no wonder that his mind and body are rebelling. After handling an extremely demanding job, he comes home to a fussy baby, a wife in night school and mountains of bills and paperwork to do. On weekends he is rebuilding his run-down house! Finally, Jack made it clear that he and his wife have no time alone together, no fun in their lives, no social life, no regular exercise, and no escape from the baby. No wonder!!

In addition to his other pressures, Jack can't even get an uninterrupted night's sleep. He climbs into bed about midnight, but is awakened at least twice before morning. That is probably the key to his depression. Some individuals are extremely vulnerable to loss of sleep and this man appears to be one of them. I am another. Our son, Ryan, did not sleep through the night once in his first four months, and I thought I was going to die. Do you remember what that was like with your newborns? There is no sound on earth quite like the piercing screech of an infant in the wee small hours of the morning. (Incidentally, people who say they "sleep like a baby" probably never had one.)

It may be impossible for this family to make immediate and sweeping changes in their lifestyle, but that's what is necessary to avoid greater problems. Margie is coping for the moment, but she will eventually crack too. I would recommend for starters that they postpone reconstructing their house, spending that money instead on childcare and weekend trips to the mountains or beach. They both desperately need at least one day a week away from the baby. Breast-feeding is a problem, but there are solutions to it. Will the child scream when they leave? Yes. Will that hurt him? Not nearly as much as having parents who are too worn out to care for him.

Transition

What will happen if this couple does not find some source of relief? Well, fortunately, their baby will not always be so demanding. But toddlerhood lies ahead and new babies are always a possibility. If they continue to give out without taking in, they will slide from the second stage of burnout into the third. According to Procaccini and Kiefaber, this is the most critical phase. They called it the *transition stage* because decisions are usually made during this period that will determine the well-being of the family for years to come. They will either recognize the downward path they are on and make changes to reverse it, or else they will continue their plunge toward chaos.

What is felt during this third stage is indescribable fatigue, self-condemnation, great anger, and resentment. For the first time, a couple in this situation openly blames the kids for their discontent. One of the reasons they were so excited about parenthood was their idealistic expectation of what children are like. They honestly did not know that little boys and girls can be, and usually are, demanding, self-centered, sloppy, lazy, and rebellious. It wasn't supposed to be this way! In fact, they expected the kids to meet *their* needs for love and appreciation. Instead it is give! give! give! take! take! take! Depression and tears are daily visitors.

Pulling Away

The human mind will not tolerate that level of agitation for very long. It will seek to protect itself from further pain. As indicated earlier, this transition phase usually leads either to beneficial changes or to a destructive self-defense. The latter occurs in Stage Four, which the authors call pulling away. The individual withdraws from the family and becomes "unavailable" to the children. The mother may not even hear them, even though they tug at her skirt and beg for her attention. She may slip into alcoholism or drug or tranquilizer abuse to dull her senses further. If forced to deal with the minor accidents and irritants of childhood, such as spilled milk or glue on the carpet, she may overreact violently and punish wildly. Fantasies of "slinging the brat against the wall" or "bashing him good" may recur in this angry and guilt-ridden parent. Obviously, child abuse is only an inch away. It occurs thousands of times daily in most Western countries.

If asked to explain what she is feeling, a mother in the fourth stage of burnout will say something like this, "I just can't deal with the kids right now." I counseled a woman in this situation who told me, referring to her children, "They hang around my ankles and beg for this or that, but I'll tell you, I kick 'em off. I'm not going to let 'em destroy my life!" She was a living, breathing stick of dynamite waiting to be ignited. People who reach this stage not only pull away from their children, but they tend to become isolated from their spouses and other family members too. Thus, being physically and psychologically exhausted, guilt-ridden to the core, drenched in self-hatred and disappointed with life, these parents descend into the fifth stage of burnout.

The Final Phase

The final phase is called *chronic disenchantment* by Procaccini and Kiefaber. It is characterized by confusion and apathy. The individual at this stage has lost all meaning and purpose in living. Identity is blurred. Weeks may pass with nothing of significance being remembered. Sexual desire is gone and the marriage is seriously troubled. Recurring thoughts may focus on suicide, "cracking up," or running away. Clearly, this individual is desperately in need of counseling and a radical shift in lifestyle. If nothing changes, neither generation will ever be quite the same again.

And it is all so unnecessary!

Now let's take a closer look at the typical home today. Most of my readers will never reach the latter stages of burnout described above. Life is hard, but it isn't *that* hard. Some of you, however, will spend your parenting years in a state of general fatigue and stress, perhaps characterized by stage two. You'll crowd your days with junk . . . with unnecessary responsibilities and commitments that provide no lasting benefits. Precious energy resources will be squandered on that which only *seems* important at the moment. Consequently, your parenting years will pass in a blur of irritation and frustration. How can you know if this is happening even now? Well, continual screaming, nagging, threatening, punishing, criticizing, and scolding of children is a pretty sure tip-off. There must be a better way to raise our sons and daughters.

One of the most common mistakes of young families is to duplicate the error of the young father who wrote to me. Jack and Margie attempted to accomplish too much too soon. I flinch when a newly married couple tells me they intend during their first two years together to go to school, have a baby, work full time, fix up a house, moonlight for extra money, and teach Sunday school class.

It is a hairbrained plan. The human body will not tolerate that kind of pressure. And when one's body is finally exhausted, an interesting thing happens to the emotions. They also malfunction.

You see, the mind, body, and spirit are very close

neighbors and one usually catches the ills of the other. You'll recall that Jack did not understand his depression. He had every reason to be happy. He was miserable. Why? Because his depleted physical condition greatly affected his mental apparatus. And if the truth were known, his spiritual life probably wasn't all that inspiring either. The three departments of our intellectual apparatus are tightly linked and they tend to move up and down as a unit. (Remember how Elijah became depressed and wanted to die immediately after his exhausting confrontation with the prophets of Baal?) This is why it is so important for us to maintain and support the triad: mind, body, and spirit. If one breaks down, the entire engine begins to sputter.

In summary, I join the authors of *Parent Burnout* in urging you to use your physical resources carefully and wisely in the years ahead. Raising children is not unlike a long-distance race in which the contestants must learn to pace themselves. If you blast out of the blocks as though you were running a sprint, you will inevitably tire out. You'll gasp and stumble as the road winds endlessly before you. Then when you come to heartbreak hill, better known as adolescence, there will be no reserve with which to finish the course. Parenting, you see, is a marathon, and we have to adopt a pace that we can maintain for two or even three decades. That is the secret of winning.

A balanced life makes that possible!

---

[1] Copyright © 1987, Dr. Joseph Procaccini and Mark W. Kiefaber, *Parent Burnout,* Doubleday & Company, Inc., New York, NY 10167.

[2] Copyright © 1987, F. Turnridge, reprinted with permission.

Chapter Nine

Suggestions for Parents of Adolescents

Adolescence is a fascinating and crazy time of life. It reminds me in some ways of the very early space probes that blasted off from Cape Canaveral in Florida. I remember my excitement when Colonel John Glenn and the other astronauts embarked on their perilous journeys into space. It was a thrilling time to be an American.

People who lived through those years will recall that a period of maximum danger occurred as each spacecraft was reentering the earth's atmosphere. The flier inside was entirely dependent on the heat shield on the bottom of the capsule to protect him from temperatures in excess of one thousand degrees Fahrenheit. If the craft descended at the wrong angle, the astronaut would be burned to cinders. At that precise moment of anxiety, negative ions would accumulate around the capsule and prevent all communication with the earth for approximately seven minutes. The world waited breathlessly for news of the astronaut's safety. Presently, the reassuring voice of Chris Craft would break in to say, "This is Mission Control. We have made contact with Friendship Seven. Everything is A-Okay. Splashdown is imminent." Cheers and prayers went up in restaurants, banks, airports, and millions of homes across the country. Even Walter Cronkite seemed relieved.

The analogy to adolescence is not so difficult to recognize. After the training and preparation of childhood are over, a pubescent youngster marches out to the launching pad. His parents watch apprehensively as he climbs aboard a capsule called adolescence and waits for his rockets to fire. His father and mother wish they could go with him, but there is room for just one person in the spacecraft. Besides, nobody invited them. Without warning, the mighty rocket engines begin to roar and the "umbilical cord" falls away. "Liftoff! We have liftoff!" screams the boy's father.

Junior, who was a baby only yesterday, is on his way to the edge of the universe. A few weeks later, his parents go through the scariest experience of their lives: They suddenly lose all contact with the capsule. "Negative ions" have interfered with communication at a time when they most want to be assured of their son's safety. Why won't he talk to them?

This period of silence does not last a few minutes, as it did with Colonel Glenn and friends. It may continue for years. The same kid who used to talk a mile a minute and ask a million questions has now reduced his vocabulary to nine monosyllabic phrases. They are, "I dunno," "Maybe," "I forget," "Huh?," "No!," "Nope," "Yeah," "Who—me?" and "He did it." Otherwise, only "static" comes through the receivers—groans, grunts, growls, and gripes. What an apprehensive time it is for those who wait on the ground!

Years later when Mission Control believes the space-craft to have been lost, a few scratchy signals are picked up unexpectedly from a distant transmitter. The parents are jubilant as they hover near their radio. Was that *really* his voice? It is deeper and more mature than they remembered. There it is again. This time the intent is unmistakable. Their spacey son has made a deliber-ate effort to correspond with them! He was fourteen years old when he blasted into space and now he is nearly twenty. Could it be that the negative environ-ment has been swept away and communication is again possible? Yes. For most families, that is precisely what happens. After years of quiet anxiety, parents learn to their great relief that everything is A-Okay on board the spacecraft. The "splashdown" occurring during the early twenties can then be a wonderful time of life for both generations.

Isn't there some way to avoid this blackout period and the other stresses associated with the adolescent voyage? Not with some teenagers, perhaps the majority. It hap-pens in the most loving and intelligent of families. Why? Because of two powerful forces that overtake and pos-sess boys and girls in the early pubescent years. Let's talk about them.

The *first* and most important is hormonal in nature. I believe parents and even behavioral scientists have underestimated the impact of the biochemical changes occurring in puberty. We can see the effect of these hor-mones on the physical body, but something equally dynamic is occurring in the brain. How else can we explain why a happy, contented, cooperative twelve-year-old *suddenly* becomes a sullen, angry, depressed thirteen-year-old? Some authorities would contend that social pressure alone accounts for this transformation. I simply don't believe that.

The emotional characteristics of a suddenly rebellious teenager are rather like the symptoms of premenstrual syndrome or severe menopause in women, or perhaps a tumultuous midlife crisis in men. Obviously, dramatic changes are going on inside! Furthermore, if the upheaval were caused entirely by environmental factors, its onset would not be so predictable in puberty. The emotional changes I have described arrive right on schedule, timed to coincide precisely with the arrival of physical maturation. Both characteristics, I contend, are driven by a common hormonal assault. Human chemistry apparently goes haywire for a few years, affecting mind as much as body.

If that explanation is accurate, then what implications does it have for parents of early adolescents? First, understanding this glandular upheaval makes it easier to tolerate and cope with the emotional reverberations that are occurring. For several years, some kids are not entirely rational! Just as a severely menopausal woman may accuse her innocent and bewildered husband of infidelity, a hormonally depressed teenager may not interpret his world accurately, either. His social judgment is impaired. Therefore, don't despair when it looks like everything you have tried to teach your kid seems to have been forgotten. He is going through a metamorphosis that has turned everything upside down. But stick around. He'll get his legs under him again!

I strongly recommend that parents of strong-willed and rebellious females quietly plot the particulars of her menstrual cycle. Not only should you record when her period begins and ends each month, but also make a comment or two each day about her mood. I think you will see that the emotional blowups that tear the family apart are cyclical in nature. Premenstrual tension at that age can produce a flurry of tornadoes every twenty-eight days. If you know they are coming, you can retreat to the storm cellar when the wind begins to blow. You can also use this record to teach your girls about premenstrual syndrome and how to cope with it. Unfortunately, many parents never seem to notice the regularity and pre-dictability of severe conflict with their daughters. Again, I recommend that you watch the calendar. It will tell you so much about your girls.

Emotional balance in teenage boys is not so cyclical, but their behavior is equally influenced by hormones. Everything from sexual passion to aggressiveness is motivated by the new chemicals that surge through their veins.

I indicated that there were two great forces which combine to create havoc during adolescence, the first having an hormonal origin. The other is social in nature. It is common knowledge that a twelve- or thirteen-year-old child suddenly awakens to a brand-new world around him, as though his eyes were opening for the first time. That world is populated by agemates who scare him out of his wits. His greatest anxiety, far exceeding the fear of death, is the possibility of rejection or humiliation in the eyes of his peers. This ultimate danger will lurk in the background for years, motivating him to do things that make absolutely no sense to the adults who watch. It is impossible to comprehend the adolescent mind without understanding this terror of the peer group.

I'll never forget a vulnerable girl named Lisa who was a student when I was in high school. She attended modern-dance classes and was asked to perform during an all-school assembly program. Lisa was in the ninth grade and had not begun to develop sexually. As she spun around the stage that day, the unthinkable happened! The top to her strapless blouse suddenly let go (it had nothing to grip) and dropped to her waist. The student body gasped and then roared with laughter. It was terrible! Lisa stood clutching frantically at her bare body for a moment and then fled from the stage in tears. She never fully recovered from the tragedy. And you can bet that her "friends" made sure she remembered it for the rest of her life.

Such a situation would also humiliate an adult, of course, but it was worse for a teenager like Lisa. An embarrassment of that magnitude could even take away the desire to live, and indeed, thousands of adolescents are killing themselves every year. We must ask ourselves, why? How do we explain this paralyzing social fear at an age when other kinds of dangers are accepted in stride? Teenagers are known to be risktakers. They drive their cars like maniacs and their record for bravery in combat ranks among the best. Why, then, can an eighteen-year-old be taught to attack an enemy gun emplacement or run through a minefield, and yet he panics in the quiet company of his peers? Whence cometh this great vulnerability?

I believe the answer is to be found, again, in the

nature of *power* and how it influences behavior. Adolescent society is based on the exercise of raw force. That is the heart and soul of its value system. It comes in various forms, of course. For girls, there is no greater social dominance than physical beauty. A truly gorgeous young woman is so powerful that even the boys are often terrified of her. She rules in a high-school setting like a queen on her throne, and in fact, she is usually elected to some honor with references to royalty in its name (Homecoming Queen, All-school Queen, Sweetheart's Queen, Football Queen, etc.). The way she uses this status to intimidate her subjects is in itself a fascinating study in adolescent behavior.

Boys derive power from physical attractiveness too, but also from athletic accomplishment in certain pre-scribed sports, from owning beautiful cars and from learning to be cool under pressure. It is also a function of sheer physical strength.

Do you remember what the world of adolescence was like for you? Do you recall the power games that were played—the highly competitive and hostile environment into which you walked every day? Can you still feel the apprehension you experienced when a popular (power-ful) student called you a creep, or a jerk, or he put his big hand in your face and pushed you out of the way? He wore a football jersey which reminded you that the entire team would eat you alive if you should be so foolish as to fight back. Does the memory of the junior-senior prom still come to mind occasionally, when you were either turned down by the girl you loved or were not asked by the boy of your dreams? Have you ever had the campus heroes make fun of the one flaw you most wanted to hide, and then threaten to mangle you on the way home from school?

Perhaps you never went through these stressful encounters. Maybe you were one of the powerful elite who oppressed the rest of us. But your son or daughter could be on the other end of the continuum. A few years ago I talked to a mother whose seventh-grade daughter was getting butchered at school each day. She said the girl awakened an hour before she had to get up each morning and lay there thinking about how she could get through her day without being humiliated.

Typically, power games are more physical for adolescent males than females. The bullies literally force their wills on those who are weaker. That is what I remember most clearly from my own high school years. I had a number of fights during that era just to preserve my turf. There was one dude, however, whom I had no intention of tackling. His name was Killer McKeechern and he was the terror of the town. It was generally believed that Killer would destroy anyone who crossed him. That theory was never tested, to my knowledge. No one dared. At least, not until I blundered along.

When I was fifteen years old and an impulsive sophomore, I nearly ended a long and happy manhood before it had a chance to get started. As I recall, a blizzard had blown through our state the night before and a group of us gathered in front of the school to throw snowballs at passing cars. (Does that tell you something about our collective maturity at the time?) Just before the afternoon bell rang, I looked up the street and saw McKeechern chugging along in his "chopped" 1934 Chevy. It was a junk heap with a cardboard "window" on the driver's side.

McKeechern had cut a 3 x 3 inch flap in the cardboard, which he lifted when turning left. You could see his evil eyes peering out just before he went around corners. When the flap was down, however, he was oblivious to things on the left side of the car. As luck would have it, that's where I was standing with a huge snowball in my hand—thinking very funny and terribly unwise thoughts.

If I could just go back to that day and counsel myself, I would say, "Don't do it, Jim! You could lose your sweet life right here. McKeechern will tear your tongue out if you hit him with that snowball. Just put it down and go quietly to your afternoon class. Please, son! If *you* lose, I lose!" Unfortunately, no such advice wafted to my ears that day and I didn't have the sense to realize my danger. I heaved the snowball into the upper atmosphere with all my might. It came down just as McKeechern drove by and, unbelievably, went through the flap in his cardboard window. The missile obviously hit him squarely in the face, because his Chevy wobbled all over the road. It bounced over the curb and came to a stop just short of the Administration Building. Killer exploded from the front seat, ready to rip someone to shreds (me!). I'll never forget the sight. There was snow all over his face and little jets of steam were curling from his head. My whole life passed in front of my eyes as I faded into the crowd. *So young!* I thought.

The only thing that saved me on this snowy day was McKeechern's inability to identify me. No one told him I had thrown the snowball, and believe me, I didn't volunteer. I escaped unscathed, although that brush with destiny must have damaged me emotionally. I still have recurring nightmares about the event thirty-five years later. In my dreams, the chimes ring and I go to open the front door. There stands McKeechern with a shotgun. And he still has snow on his face. (If you read this story, Killer, I do hope we can be friends. We were only kids, you know? Right, Killer? Huh? Right! Howsa car?)

Why have I reminded you of the world of adolescent power? Because your teenagers are knee deep in it right now. That is why they are nervous wrecks on the first day of school, or before the team plays its initial game, or any other time when their power base is on the line. The raw nerve, you see, is not really dominance, but self-esteem. One's sense of worth is dependent on peer acceptance at that age, and that is why the group holds such enormous influence over the individual. If he is mocked, disrespected, ridiculed, and excluded—in other words, if he is stripped of power—his delicate ego is torn to shreds. As we have said, that is a fate worse than death itself. Social panic is the by-product of that system.

Now, what about your sons and daughters? Have you wondered why they come home from school in such a terrible mood? Have you asked them why they are so jumpy and irritable through the evening? They cannot describe their feelings to you, but they may have engaged in a form of combat all day. Even if they haven't had to fight with their fists, it is likely that they are embroiled in a highly competitive, openly hostile environment where emotional danger lurks on every side. Am I over-stating the case? Yes, for the kid who is coping well. But for the powerless young man and woman, I haven't begun to tell their stories.

To help parents cope with these special stresses of the adolescent years, let me offer five suggestions that have been beneficial to others, as follows:

1. Boredom Is Dangerous to Energetic Teenagers. Keep Them Moving.

The strong-willed adolescent simply must not be given large quantities of unstructured time. He will find destructive ways to use such moments. My advice is to get him involved in the very best church youth program you can find. If your local congregation has only four bored members in its junior high department and seven sleepy high schoolers, I would consider changing churches. I know that advice could be disruptive to the entire family and I'm sure most pastors would disagree, but you must save that volatile kid. Obviously, such radical action is not as necessary for the more compliant individual or for one who has other wholesome outlets for his energy. But if you're sitting on a keg of dynamite, you have to find ways to keep the powder dry! Not only can this be done through church activities, but also by involvement with athletics, music, horses or other animals, and part-time jobs. You must keep that strong-willed kid's scrawny legs churning!

2. Don't Rock the Boat.

In my second film series entitled, "Turn Your Heart Toward Home," I offered this advice to parents of teenagers: "Get 'em through it." That may not sound like such a stunning idea, but I believe it has merit for most families—especially those with one or more toughminded kids. The concept is a bit obscure, so I will resort to a couple of pictures to illustrate my point.

When parents of strong-willed children look ahead to the adolescent river, they often perceive it to be like the one on the following page.

In other words, they expect the early encounter with rapids to give way to swirling currents and life-threatening turbulence. If that doesn't turn over their teenagers' boat, they seem destined to drown farther downstream when they plunge over the falls.

Fortunately, the typical journey is much safer than anticipated. Most often it flows like the picture below.

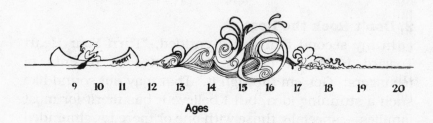

What I'm saying is that the river usually descends not into the falls but into smooth water once more. Even though your teenager may be splashing and thrashing

several hours there, I admitted to his father that I had had a bad fight with my dad and he didn't know where I was. My uncle persuaded me to call home and assure my parents that I was safe. With knees quaking, I phoned my dad.

"Stay there," he said. "I'm coming over."

To say that I was apprehensive for the next few minutes would be an understatement. In a short time Dad arrived and asked to see me alone.

"Bo," he began. "I didn't treat you right this afternoon. I was riding your back for no good reason and I want you to know I'm sorry. Your mom and I want you to come on home now."

He made a friend for life.

3. Maintain a Reserve Army.

A good military general will never commit all his troops to combat at the same time. He maintains a reserve force that can relieve the exhausted soldiers when they falter on the front lines. I wish parents of adolescents would implement the same strategy. Instead, they commit every ounce of their energy and every second of their time to the business of living, holding nothing in reserve for the challenge of the century. It is a classic mistake which can be disastrous for parents of strong-willed adolescents. Let me explain.

The problem begins with a basic misunderstanding during the preschool years. I hear mothers say, "I don't plan to work until the kids are in kindergarten. Then I'll get a job." They appear to believe that the heavy demands on them will end magically when they get their youngest in school. In reality, the teen years will generate as much pressure on them as did the preschool era. An adolescent turns a house upside down . . . literally and figuratively. Not only is the typical rebellion of those years an extremely stressful experience, but the chauffeuring, supervising, cooking, and cleaning required to support an adolescent can be exhausting. *Someone* within the family must reserve the energy to cope with those new challenges. Mom is the candidate of choice. Remember, too, that menopause and a man's midlife crisis are scheduled to coincide with adolescence, which makes a wicked soup! It is a wise mother who doesn't exhaust herself at a time when so much is going on at home.

I know it is easier to talk about maintaining a lighter schedule than it is to secure one. It is also impractical to recommend that mothers not seek formal employment during this era. Millions of women have to work for economic reasons, including the rising number of single parents in our world. Others choose to pursue busy careers. That is a decision to be made by a woman and her husband, and I would not presume to tell them what to do.

But decisions have inevitable consequences. In this case, there are biophysical forces at work which simply must be reckoned with. If, for example, 80 percent of a woman's available energy in a given day is expended in getting dressed, driving to work, doing her job for eight or ten hours, and stopping by the grocery store on the way home—then there is only 20 percent left for everything else. Maintenance of the family, cooking meals, cleaning the kitchen, relating to her husband, and all other personal activities must be powered by that diminishing resource. It is no wonder that her batteries are spent by the end of the day. Weekends should be restful, but they are usually not. Thus, she plods through the years on her way to burnout.

This is my point: A woman in this situation has thrown all her troops into front-line combat. As we saw in the previous chapter on burnout, she is already exhausted but there is no reserve on which to call. In that weakened condition, the routine stresses of raising an adolescent can be overwhelming. Let me say it again. Raising boisterous teenagers is an exciting and rewarding but also a frustrating experience. Their radical highs and lows affect our moods. The noise, the messes, the complaints, the arguments, the sibling rivalry, the missed curfews, the paced floors, the wrecked car, the failed test, the jilted lover, the wrong friends, the busy telephone, the pizza on the carpet, the ripped new blouse, the rebellion, the slammed doors, the mean words, the tears—it's enough to drive a *rested* mother crazy. But what about our career woman who already "gave at the office," then came home to this chaos? Any unexpected crisis or even a minor irritant can set off a torrent of emotion. There is no reserve on which to draw. In short, the parents of adolescents should save some energy with which to cope with aggravation!

Whether or not you are able to accept and implement my advice is your business. It is mine to offer it, and this is my best shot: To help you get through the turbulence of adolescence, you should:

1. Keep the schedule simple.
2. Get plenty of rest.
3. Eat nutritious meals.
4. Stay on your knees.

When fatigue leads adults to act like hot-tempered teenagers, anything can happen at home.

4. The Desperate Need for Fathers.

It is stating the obvious, I suppose, to say that fathers of rebellious teenagers are desperately needed at home during those years. In their absence, mothers are left to handle disciplinary problems alone. This is occurring in millions of families headed by single mothers today, and I know how tough their task has become. Not only are they doing a job that should have been shouldered by two; they must also deal with behavioral problems that fathers are more ideally suited to handle. It is generally understood that a man's larger size, deeper voice, and masculine demeanor make it easier for him to deal with defiance in the younger generation. Likewise, I believe the exercise of authority is a mantle ascribed to him by the Creator.

Not only are fathers needed to provide leadership and discipline during the adolescent years, but they can be highly influential on their sons during this period of instability. (We will discuss fathers and daughters presently.) Someone has said, "Link a boy to the right man and he seldom goes wrong." I believe that is true. If a dad and his son can develop hobbies together or other common interests, the rebellious years can pass in relative tranquility. What they experience may be remembered for a lifetime.

I recall a song, written by Dan Fogelberg, that told about a man who shared his love of music with his elderly father. It is called "Leader of the Band," and its message touches something deep within me. This is the way it should be:

An only child
Alone and wild
A cabinet maker's son
His hands were meant
For different work
And his heart was known to none—
He left his home
And went his lone
And solitary way
And he gave to me
A gift I know I never can repay.

A quiet man of music
Denied a simpler fate
He tried to be a soldier once
But his music wouldn't wait

He earned his love through discipline
A thundering, velvet hand
His gentle means of sculpting souls
Took me years to understand.

The leader of the band is tired
And his eyes are growing old
But his blood runs through my instrument
And his song is in my soul—

My life has been a poor attempt
To imitate the man
I'm just a living legacy
To the leader of the band.

My brothers' lives were different
For they heard another call
One went to Chicago

PARENTING ISN'T FOR COWARDS

And the other to St. Paul
And I'm in Colorado
When I'm not in some hotel
Living out this life I've chose
And come to know so well.

I thank you for the music
And your stories of the road
I thank you for the freedom
When it came my time to go—
I thank you for the kindness
And the times when you got tough
And, papa, I don't think I
Said "I love you" near enough—

The leader of the band is tired
And his eyes are growing old
But his blood runs through my instrument
And his song is in my soul—
My life has been a poor attempt
To imitate the man
I'm just a living legacy
To the leader of the band.
I am the living legacy to
The leader of the band.[1]

Can't you see this man going to visit his aged father today, with a lifetime of love passing between them? That must have been what God had in mind when he gave dads to boys. Let me address the reader directly: What common ground are you cultivating with *your* impressionable son? Some fathers build or repair cars with them; some construct small models or make things in a wood shop. My dad and I hunted and fished together. There is no way to describe what those days meant to me as we entered the woods in the early hours of the morning. How could I get angry at this man who took time to be with me? We had wonderful talks while coming home from a day of laughter and fun in the country.

I've tried to maintain that kind of contact with my son, Ryan. We've rebuilt a Model A Ford together. We've also hunted rabbits, quail, pheasant, and larger game since he turned twelve. As it was with my father, Ryan and I have had some meaningful conversations while out in the fields together. For example, we got up one morning and situated ourselves in a deer blind before the break of day. About twenty yards away from us was a feeder which operated on a timer. At seven A.M. it automatically dropped kernels of corn into a pan below.

Ryan and I huddled together in this blind, talking softly about whatever came to mind. Then through the fog, we saw a beautiful doe emerge silently into the clearing. She took nearly thirty minutes to get to the feeder near where we were hiding. We had no intention of shooting her, but it was fun to watch this beautiful animal from close range. She was extremely wary, sniffing the air and listening for the sounds of danger. Finally, she inched her way to the feeder, still looking around skittishly as though sensing our presence. Then she ate a quick breakfast and fled.

I whispered to Ryan, "There is something valuable to be learned from what we have just seen. Whenever you come upon a free supply of high quality corn, unexpectedly provided right there in the middle of the forest, be careful! The people who put it there are probably sitting nearby in a blind, just waiting to take a shot at you. Keep your eyes and ears open!"

Ryan may not always remember that advice, but I will. It isn't often a father says something that he considers profound to his teenage son. One thing is certain: This interchange and the other ideas we shared on that day would not have occurred at home. Opportunities for that kind of communication have to be created. And it's worth working to achieve.

Before we leave the subject of fathers interacting with their sons, I want to reflect briefly on a *mother's* contribution to that relationship. Women can help the generations bond together or they can drive a wedge between them. This concept was expressed beautifully in a book entitled *Fathers and Sons* by Lewis Yablonsky. The author observed that mothers are the *primary* interpreters of fathers' personality, character, and integrity to their sons. In other words, the way boys see their fathers is largely a product of the things their mothers have said and the way she feels. In Yablonsky's case, his mother destroyed the respect he might have had for his father. This is what he wrote:

> I vividly recall sitting at the dinner table with my two brothers and father and mother and cringing at my mother's attacks on my father. "Look at him," she would say in Yiddish. "His shoulders are bent down, he's a failure. He doesn't have the courage to get a better job or make more money. He's a beaten man." He would keep his eyes pointed toward his plate and never answer her. She never extolled his virtues or persistence or the fact that he worked so hard. Instead she

constantly focused on the negative and created an image to his three sons of a man without fight, crushed by a world over which he had no control.

His not fighting back against her constant criticism had the effect of confirming its validity to her sons. And my mother's treatment and the picture of my father did not convey to me that marriage was a happy state of being, or that women were basically people. I was not especially motivated to assume the role of husband and father myself from my observations of my whipped father.

My overall research clearly supports that the mother is the basic filter and has enormous significance in the father-son relationship.[2]

Though Yablonsky did not say so, it is also true that fathers can do great damage to the conception their children may have of their mother. Very early on I found that when I was irritated with Shirley for some reason, my attitude was instantly picked up by our son and daughter. They seemed to feel, "If Dad can argue with Mom, then we can too." It became clear to me just how important it was for me to express my love and admiration for Shirley. However, I could *never* do that job of building respect for my wife as well as she did for me! She made me a king in my own home. If our son and daughter believed half of what she told them about me, I would have been a fortunate man. The close relationship I enjoy with Danae and Ryan today is largely a product of Shirley's great love for me and the way she "interpreted" me to our kids. I will always be grateful to her for doing that!

Fathers and Daughters

Let's talk now about fathers and daughters. Most psychologists believe, and I am one of them, that all future romantic relationships to occur in a girl's life will be influenced positively or negatively by the way she perceives and interacts with her dad. If he is an alcoholic and a bum, she will spend her life trying to replace him in her heart. If he is warm and nurturing, she will look for a lover to equal him. If he thinks she is beautiful, worthy, and feminine, she will be inclined to see herself that way. But if he rejects her as unattractive and uninteresting, she is likely to carry self-esteem problems into her adult years.

I have also observed that a woman's willingness to accept the loving leadership of her husband is significantly influenced by the way she perceived the authority of her father. If he was overbearing, uncaring, or capricious during her developmental years, she may attempt to grab the reins of leadership from her future husband. But if dad blended love and discipline in a way that conveyed strength, she will be more willing to yield to the confident leadership of her husband.

None of these tendencies or trends is absolute, of course. Individual differences can always produce exceptions and contradictions. But this statement will be hard to refute: a good father will leave his imprint on his daughter for the rest of her life.

Many fathers are also called upon to perform another vitally important role during the adolescent years. It occurs when tension begins to develop between mothers and teenage girls. That conflict is very common among the ladies of the house, and as you recall, it showed up in the findings from our study of temperaments. Several years may pass when they don't even *like* each other very much.

In that setting, fathers are desperately needed as peacemakers and mediators. I have found that teenagers who are greatly irritated with one parent will sometimes seek to preserve their relationship with the other. It's like a country at war in search of supportive allies. If fathers are chosen in that triangle, they can use the opportunity to settle their daughters and "interpret" their mothers in a more favorable light. They may also be able to help their wives ventilate their anger and understand their role in perpetuating the conflict. Without this masculine influence, routine skirmishes can turn into World War III.

In conclusion, I have this recurring message for today's fathers—especially to those who have teenagers at home: Don't let these years get away from you. Your contributions to your kids could rank as your greatest accomplishments in life—or your most oppressive failures. If you're not yet convinced of your importance at home, read the article that follows. If it doesn't touch your heart you may not have one.

Dad Coming Home Was the Real Treat

by Howard Mann

When I was a little boy I never left the house without kissing my parents goodbye.

I liked kissing my mother because her cheek felt mushy and warm, and because she smelled of peppermints. I liked kissing my father because he felt rough and whiskery and smelled of cigars and witch hazel.

PARENTING ISN'T FOR COWARDS

About the time I was 10 years old, I came to the conclusion that I was now too big to kiss my father. A mother, OK. But with a father, a big boy should shake hands—man to man, you see.

He didn't seem to notice the difference or to mind it. Anyway, he never said anything about it. But then he never said much about anything, except his business.

In retrospect, I guess it was also my way of getting even with him. Up until then, I had always felt I was something special to him. Every day, he would come home from that mysterious world of his with a wondrous treat, just for me. It might be a miniature baseball bat, engraved with Babe Ruth's signature. It might be a real honeycomb with waffle-like squares soaked in honey. Or it might be exotic rahat, the delectable, jellied Turkish candies, buried in powdered sugar and crowded into a little wooden crate.

How I looked forward to his coming home each night! The door flung open and there he stood. I would run to him, hug him while he lifted me high in his arms.

I reached my peak the day of my seventh birthday. I woke up before anyone else in the family and tiptoed into the dining room. There, on the heavy mahogany table, was a small, square wristwatch with a brown leather strap, stretched out full length in a black velvet box. Could it really be for me? I picked it up and held it to my ear. It ticked! Not a toy watch from the 5-and-10, but a real watch like grown-ups wore. I ran into his bedroom, woke up Father and covered him with kisses. Could any boy possibly be as happy as me?

Later, it began to change. At first, I wasn't aware it was happening. I supposed I was too busy with school and play and having to make new friends all the time. (We moved every two years, always seeking a lower rent.)

The flow of treats dried up. No more bats or honeycombs. My father gradually disappeared from my life. He would come home late, long after I had gone to sleep. And he would come home with his hands empty. I missed him very much, but I was afraid to say anything. I hoped that he would come back to me as strangely as he had left. Anyhow, big boys weren't supposed to long for their fathers.

Years after he died, my mother talked about how the Depression had "taken the life out of him." It had crushed his dream of being a "big man." He no longer had money for treats. He no longer had time for me.

I am sorry now. I look at his picture and his crinkly hazel eyes and wish that he were here today. I would tell him what is happening with me now and talk about things that he might like to hear—politics, foreign events and how business is doing. And I would put my arms around his neck and say, "Pop, you don't have to bring me anything—just come home early." And I would kiss him. [3]

5. Handling the Very Toughest Cases.

Go back with me now to the story I told about my dad's apology during our brief disagreement in the backyard. He took all the blame for that confrontation and in essence, "ate humble pie." I must make it clear that it is not always wise to assume this posture. In fact, I believe most parents of very difficult teenagers go too far in that direction. There is a time for parents to get off their knees and *quit* apologizing. They have sought to avoid conflict by groveling and appeasing their strong-willed adolescents, and in so doing, they have made what turns out to be a tragic mistake. Please remember this fact: To a power-hungry tyrant of any age, appeasement only inflames his lust for more power. Behavioral research has now demonstrated this relationship between insecure, permissive parents and violent, delinquent teenagers.

Dr. Henry Harbin and Dr. Denis Madden observed a significant increase in the number of vicious attacks on parents by their unruly children. Working at the University of Maryland's Medical School, these psychiatrists also studied the circumstances surrounding this form of family violence. Surprisingly, they found that "parent battering" usually occurs when "one or both parents have abdicated the executive position" and when no one is in charge. No one, that is, except possibly the violent child.

Harbin and Madden also observed that "an almost universal element" in the parent-battering cases was the parents' unwillingness to admit the seriousness of the situation. They did not call the police, even when their lives were in danger; they lied to protect the children and they continued to give in to their demands. Parental authority had collapsed.

One father was almost killed when his angry son pushed him down a flight of stairs. He insisted that the boy did not have a bad temper. Another woman was stabbed by her son, missing her heart by an inch. Nevertheless, she continued letting him live at home.

Drs. Harbin and Madden concluded that appeasement and permissiveness are related to youthful violence, and that both parents should lead with firmness. "Someone needs to be in charge," they said.[4]

Obviously, I agree wholeheartedly with these psychiatrists. Having been appointed by President Ronald Reagan to serve on the National Advisory Commission to the Office of Juvenile Justice and Delinquency Prevention, I am very familiar with the pattern of youthful violence. I've seen cold-blooded killers who were no more than thirteen years of age. Many of them came from homes where authority was weak or nonexistent. It is a formula for cranking out very tough criminals at an early age.

That brings us to the most difficult question with which parents are ever confronted: What can be done in those cases when parental leadership collapses altogether? What resources are available to mothers and fathers when an adolescent continually breaks the law, intimidates or attacks his family, and does precisely what he wishes? If appeasement makes matters worse, as we have seen, what other approaches can we suggest?

Though it would be glib to imply that there are simple answers to such awesome questions, I believe one organization is on the right track. It is called TOUGHLOVE, founded by Phyllis and David York. TOUGHLOVE is dedicated to helping out-of-control parents regain the upper hand in their own homes. Their basic philosophy is one of confrontation that is designed to bring a belligerent teenager to his senses.

The TOUGHLOVE concept began during the early 1980s, after counselors Phyllis and David York had run into serious problems with their eighteen-year-old daughter. She broke every rule and eventually held up a cocaine dealer in Landsdale, Pennsylvania. She was soon arrested at gunpoint in the Yorks' home. That got their attention.

From this painful experience, the Yorks began to formulate the TOUGHLOVE principles. They are simple enough: forgiveness and understanding are laudable responses to defiance, but they do not work with the most difficult cases. As York said, "I started out being this nice therapist. 'Let me listen, let me be this daddy to you guys.' And what really needs to happen is to grab these kids and say, 'You really can't do that. You've got to follow the rules here, and if you don't we're going to call the police and have you locked up!'"

Instead of groveling and whining, parents of rebellious teens are encouraged to stand firm and take appropriate action. This may include taking away the family car, restricting use of the telephone, and refusing to intervene when the teen is in jail. It may also involve locking a drug user out of his home. A note on the front door informs him that he will be welcome there only if he enrolls in a drug-rehab program. A teen who comes home hours after his curfew may find a note instructing him to spend the night with another family that is willing to take him in.

Time magazine, 8 June 1981, quoted TOUGHLOVE mothers as follows, "It's just old-fashioned discipline, where the parents run the home and there is cooperation among the family members." Another said she turned in her son, Jeff, 17, to the police after he confessed to robbing a nearby home to support his drug habit. "Police enrolled him in a rehabilitation program," said *Time*, "and now he is back home, working and attending Narcotics and Alcoholics Anonymous."

Many similar examples are cited in the Yorks' book

Toughlove. But as might be expected, most parents lack the confidence and understanding needed to implement the principles on their own. They need the support of other parents who are going through the same trauma. That's why the TOUGHLOVE organization was founded. It puts harassed parents in touch with one another. Then if a teenager is sent to prison, for example, his distressed mother and father may ask other members of their local TOUGHLOVE group to visit him first, or to accompany them to the prison. It is an idea whose time has come.

The article in *Time* magazine concluded with this statement:

> TOUGHLOVE brings parents together to buck up one another at meetings and to follow the progress of problem youngsters. If a runaway is picked up in another state or a youngster is arrested, members in the group are ready to go to the scene. Says Ted Wachtel, president of the Community Service Foundation in Sellersville, Pa., which sponsors the TOUGHLOVE movement: "If a child winds up in prison, it is sometimes too much of an emotional experience for the parents to go at first, so other members of the group make the visits."
>
> TOUGHLOVE does not work all the time, but so far it has been an effective way of uniting parents to square off against the youngsters' own powerful peer group that endorses drug taking and rebelliousness. One tactic of TOUGHLOVE is to make a list of a youngster's closest friends, then go out and meet the parents of the friends and try to make an alliance. The message: Don't feel guilty; don't get into shouting matches with youngsters;

don't be a victim; get over disillusionment. Says the TOUGHLOVE self-help manual for parents: "We really were not prepared for such a rapidly changing culture full of distractions like dope, violence, and a peer group that means more to our children than a home and family." In TOUGHLOVE'S view, the time has come for parents to stand up against a hostile culture.[5]

What has been the public response to the TOUGH-LOVE concept? There were twenty-five groups scattered around the United States in 1981. Today there are more than fifteen hundred in all fifty states and in Canada. It has become a national movement.

If you are among those fed-up parents who have reached the end of your rope, you might want to contact TOUGHLOVE'S national headquarters. Their address is:

TOUGHLOVE INTERNATIONAL
P.O. Box 1069
Doylestown, PA 18901
(800) 333-1069

Do I recommend them personally? Yes, with two reservations: (1) TOUGHLOVE is not a Christian organization, although I have not known them to contradict our basic beliefs. I wish a similar national program existed that emphasized prayer and Scripture, but I know of none. In the meantime, TOUGHLOVE is getting the job done. (2) Any franchised program like this will be no better than the people who operate it on a local level. You could get a lemon, so to speak. I will say this, however: I have heard very little criticism of the TOUGHLOVE program in all these years. Hundreds of grateful parents wrote to me after the Yorks were guests on our Focus on the Family radio broadcast. One woman told our program director, "TOUGHLOVE literally saved my life. I would not have survived without it."

Whether or not you are in need of the radical support provided by TOUGHLOVE, I invite you to read an interesting article written about it by columnist Ann Landers. This article was also published in 1981, the year TOUGHLOVE burst on the scene, and was originally incorporated in *Family Circle* magazine, November 3 of that year. Note the similarity in philosophy to what we have been discussing throughout this book. Obviously, I do not agree with Landers's criticism of the Bible, and I will deal with her misinterpretation of Proverbs 22:6 in the upcoming question-and-answer chapter.

Here's the way Ann Landers sees it:

> I never thought I'd live to see the day when I'd actually argue with the Bible . . . especially since I've frequently quoted the very passage I no longer feel applies "Train up a child in the way he should go . . . and . . . he will not depart from it, meaning that if you carefully train your child, he or she will turn out well. Yet, unfortunately, the last 15 years have produced a great deal of evidence disproving this biblical directive. My desk is groaning from the weight of letters that sound a lot like this one.
>
> > Dear Ann Landers:
> >
> > We took our children to church, we didn't send them. We never had sitters. If we couldn't get his mother or mine to stay, the

children came with us or we didn't go. We invested so much love and time and energy in our sons and daughters, yet they became involved with truancy, drugs, shoplifting, a pregnancy—every kind of trouble you might expect from street kids. What went wrong?

Being a firm believer that the twigs grew in the direction they were bent, I didn't know how to respond to these anguished, guilt-ridden parents. Their letters describing years of tender loving care didn't square with what was happening to their children. Many carefully nurtured twigs seemed to be growing in bizarre and unpredictable directions. I had to rethink my answers and come up with something better.

A few years ago I printed a letter that said volumes. It was from a high school student who came across her mother's diary; the letter contained an entry the mother had written:

> All adolescent kids have diaries these days. Well, I think it's time for mothers to have diaries, too. We ought to keep a daily chronicle reporting the heartaches of parents who did the best they could with their mixed-up sons and daughters. Only the kids suffer, do they? Only their feelings are hurt? Well, move over, children, your parents are having a very hard time trying to bring you up to be self-reliant, decent citizens. It seems like the cards are stacked against us. The more we give, the less we get back.

What's gone wrong? Obviously something has. I don't pretend to know all the answers, but after reading thousands of letters from teenagers in trouble, teachers who see them almost every day, guidance counselors who listen to them, and parents who are wringing their hands in despair, I have concluded that peer pressure is a far more dominant factor in shaping teenage behavior than parental influence.

The experts with whom I checked (juvenile authorities, drug-abuse and mental-health counselors, some psychologists, a few psychiatrists) supported my notion. I'm not suggesting that parental training and role models mean nothing. What I am saying is that in our present-day culture what a teenager's peers think of him carries more weight than what his parents say.

The need to be accepted, the fear of being outside the charmed circle, the desire to be "in" is vitally important to adolescents today. And, all too often that means keg parties, getting drunk, smoking dope, popping uppers and downers, snorting cocaine, using angel dust and acid, and having sex.

Moreover, a generation that has grown up with its eyeballs hooked onto a TV screen is constantly searching for ways to combat boredom and anesthetize themselves against the pain of growing up. Teenagers (and adults, as well) have discovered that alcohol and drugs can put troubles on the back burner and make you feel "different."

According to a report put out in 1980 by the Department of Health, Education and Welfare (now called Department of Health and Human Services), one out of 10 high school students regularly uses pot. This

173

means these kids smoke at least one or two joints every day. I happen to believe that this figure is too low. High school teachers have written to tell me that on Monday mornings, at least one-third of the juniors and seniors walk into classrooms stoned. An even more frightening fact is that some of these students drive themselves to school, which helps explain why auto accidents are today's leading cause of death among teenagers. And emergency room attendants tell us that approximately 65 percent of all fatal teenage accidents are alcohol or drug-related.

How can parents combat outside influences that run counter to everything they have tried to teach their children? What advice do I have for them? Plenty. And I've already had responses telling me it works. The following letter opened my eyes and sent me in a completely new direction. It came from Bucks County, Pennsylvania.

Dear Ann:

Please print this for parents with unreachable, mixed-up, always-in-trouble teenagers. I know where they are coming from. My husband and I have been there and there's no hell like it.

We, too, were desperate and without hope. Our son was a bum, in debt, stealing from us, on drugs, breaking up the furniture, cursing and hitting us. We were beside ourselves with anxiety and fear. We tried everything to please him, and nothing worked. The nicer we were, the worse he got.

Finally we called the police. They gave us the phone number of an organization called TOUGHLOVE. From that day on we became members of a community network of parents who are successfully coping with their kids' hostile, antisocial behavior.

Before we came to TOUGHLOVE, we were ashamed and felt weak and guilty because we couldn't stand up to our son. We thought that no other parents in the community had failed as miserably as we had. Then we met other members of TOUGHLOVE and discovered that we were no longer helpless. We had the support of other parents, the police, the schools, the courts, and rehabilitation facilities.

We didn't have to throw our son out of the house, nor did we have to continue to take his abuse. We laid down a whole new set of rules and gave him a choice. He could live by our rules or get out. He chose to stay.

I'm enclosing a pamphlet that tells you more about TOUGHLOVE. Please, Ann, share it with your readers. It's the greatest thing that happened to us and we want to spread the word. Thanks for your help.

Forever Grateful

I read the pamphlet and it made a lot of sense. It explained a program designed to help parents who feel heartsick and helpless about their teenagers. The program asks parents to choose which road they want to take. Will it be confrontation, firm guidelines and mutual respect—or excuses (as usual), denial, gutlessness, continued indulgence and bribery? It encourages parents to meet the crisis head on, take a stand and demand cooperation.

Actually, the permissive method of child-rearing surfaced in the '40s, blossomed in the '50s and gained total respectability in the '60s. Psychiatrists and psychologists told us that if we spoke softly to our children; held, rocked and cuddled them; let them stop soiling their diapers and panties when they decided it was time to stop; allowed them to get the anger out of their systems, being careful never to say, "No, you can't do that" unless they started to burn down the house, they would develop healthy egos and grow up to be well-adjusted young men and women, self-assured, highly motivated and a joy to us.

We beat down our natural instincts, slavishly adhered to the teachings of these "experts" and developed dark circles and high blood pressure while our kids talked back to us, spit on us, hit us, broke their toys and threw themselves in the aisles of supermarkets (or department stores) until they got their way. These same kids turned out to be selfish, spoiled, hostile, disrespectful, lazy, and unmotivated. They had no respect for us, their teachers, or the law.

To add insult to injury, some psychiatrists charged up to $100 an hour to tell us, "There are no bad children . . . only bad parents."

The sad truth of the matter is that for too many years parents have been bamboozled by "experts," and have sopped up half-baked theories in "how-to" books instead of using the brains God gave them and reacting to their natural instincts when their kids pushed them too far in an attempt to test limits.

I'll never forget a letter I received from a 19-year-old just three years ago. She had no friends and couldn't hold a job because she was always shooting her mouth off, telling acquaintances, colleagues and bosses exactly what she thought of them. "I was brought up that way. . . " she declared. "I was allowed to say anything to any-body. My parents raised me that way and now I am all messed up and it's their fault. Any suggestions, Ann?"

I replied, "Yes . . . accept responsibility and quit blaming your parents for your mean mouth and foul moods. If you don't like the way you are—go to work on yourself and become something different. Enough of this 'You damaged me. Now take care of me' nonsense. It's a cop-out. Guilt laid on parents by you kids is so thick you can cut it with a knife—and all it does is per-petuate financial and emotional dependence and create a climate of hostility and ultimate failure."

So what can parents do with kids who have them backed against the wall? They can make a 180-degree turn and go the TOUGHLOVE route. Heaven knows reasoning, pleading, crying, threatening, and bribing hasn't worked. It's time to try something else, and I believe self-help groups like TOUGHLOVE are the most effective approach to problemsolving.

People who have shared the same problems and tri-umphed over them give one another tremendous strength. They say, "I did it; you can do it too. I'll help show you how."

Parents today encounter the following problems all too often. You are confused when your teenager comes home in varying states of intoxication or completely stoned—yet denies he's had alcohol or dope even though you've found drug paraphernalia in his room. You're heartsick and don't know what to do because your child is failing in school. Your 15-year-old takes things that belong to others. Your sophomore student lives in a filthy room and refuses to do any chores in the house. Your star-athlete son gets into trouble with the law. Your daughter stays out past curfew.

So mothers and fathers ask themselves why they're such rotten parents and say, "I'd like to kill that kid for putting us through this" . . . or, "A lot of our friends have the same trouble, they just don't talk about it." Or, "It's all our fault, so now we have to take care of them."

Bullfeathers!!!!!!!!!

You need TOUGHLOVE if you feel helpless and unable to cope with your teenagers' behavior or if you feel victimized by them, disappointed in yourself as a parent, guilty because you think you have done a rotten job and are frightened by the potential for violence in yourself and your children. These feelings are experienced by the affluent, the disadvantaged, middle income families, the uneducated, intellectual, single, divorced, married, permissive, repressive, black and white. Anybody.

Remember, you have the right to a night's sleep without worrying where your kid is—or being awakened by a phone call from the police or a hospital or a drunk teenager who's stranded somewhere. It's time you started taking care of yourself and letting your teenager be responsible for his or her actions. That's where the concepts of TOUGHLOVE come in.

You must find the courage to withdraw your money, influence, affection, anger, guilt and pleas that he or she learn to shape up. You must begin to make real demands entailing severe consequences. You must make it clear that you will not live in a house with people who mistreat you and do not respect the rules you have laid down. You do not need your teenager's approval. You're the boss. The sooner your youngster understands this, the better.

Of course, after years of accepting blame and guilt laid on by some psychiatrists, it's not easy to make this turn-about alone. You'll need help. Telephone the parents of your kids' friends. Tell them, "I'm worried about my children's behavior. Will you come to a meeting at my house tonight?" They'll probably say, "Thank heaven you called. I have been worried sick about mine too."

Call your neighbors even if they don't have children. You'll need allies in this battle and they can help. Call an understanding clergyman and sympathetic schoolteachers. Call those you know who work with delinquent children. They know the ropes.

Once you start a support group, other parents will want to join. Your local school may become interested. They're just as eager as you are to learn how to deal with difficult kids. Never in the history of our country has there been so much trouble disciplining children. Last year there were over 70,000 assaults on teachers in our public schools. When principals and teachers learn that parents are banding together to demand that their kids be respectful, law-abiding citizens, they'll want to be part of this effort.

Of course, it's unrealistic to expect unruly, anti-social children to change overnight. Some will become extremely hostile and resentful when they discover they are no longer in control. This is where the support of friends and neighbors comes in.

When Johnny does not come home at midnight, which was the curfew you laid down, lock the door and bolt it. Tack a note on the outside saying, "It's past midnight. You are not welcome here. Go to the Pattersons or the Smiths or some other neighbors.

Arrange with these people to take your kid when he breaks the house rules. Agree to take their kids when they do the same. Often teenagers will talk more easily with their friends' parents than with their own. This can be an excellent beginning. Then negotiate with the Pattersons or Smiths about the terms under which Johnny will be allowed to return home.

Not all kids are in trouble. We see many children who are law-abiding, generous, kind and a pleasure to have around. They're not spaced out on drugs; they're not running away from home and they're not driving their parents crazy. Chances are that these children were not raised by books. They were raised according to clearly defined guidelines. If they went beyond these guidelines, the consequences were sure and swift.

If you have a kid in trouble whom you've always catered to, don't feel guilty. Most of the child-rearing teachings of the past two years encouraged parents to treat children as equals and let them learn by doing their own thing.

Remember, too, as I said earlier—peer pressure means more to most children than what their parents and gasping for air, it is not likely that his boat will capsize. It is more buoyant than you might think. Yes, a few individuals do go over the falls, usually because of drug abuse. Even some of them climb back in the canoe and paddle on down the river. In fact, the greatest danger of sinking the boat could come from . . . *you!*

This warning is addressed particularly to idealistic and perfectionistic parents who are determined to make their adolescents—*all* of them—perform and achieve and measure up to the highest standard. A perfectionist, by the way, is a person who takes great pains with what he does and then gives them to everyone else. In so doing, he rocks a boat that is already threatened by the rapids. Perhaps another child could handle the additional turbulence, but our concern is for the unsteady kid—the one who lacks common sense for a while and may even lean toward irrational behavior. Don't unsettle his boat any more than you must!

I'm reminded of a waitress who recognized me when I came into the restaurant where she worked. She was not busy that day and wanted to talk about her twelve-year-old daughter. As a single mother, she had gone through severe struggles with the girl, whom she identified as being *very* strong-willed.

"We have fought tooth and nail for this entire year," she said. "It has been awful! We argue nearly every night, and most of our fights are over the same issue."

I asked her what had caused the conflict, and she replied, "My daughter is still a little girl but she wants to shave her legs. I feel she's too young to be doing that and she becomes so angry that she won't even talk to me. This has been the worst year of our lives together."

I looked at the waitress and exclaimed, "Lady, buy your daughter a razor!"

That twelve-year-old girl was paddling into a time of life that would rock her canoe good and hard. As a single parent, Mom would soon be trying to keep this rebellious kid from getting into drugs, alcohol, sex and pregnancy, early marriage, school failure, and the possibility of running away. Truly, there would be many ravenous alligators in her river within a year or two. In that setting, it seemed unwise to make a big deal over what was essentially a nonissue. While I agreed with the mother that adolescence should not be rushed into prematurely, there were higher goals than maintaining a proper developmental timetable.

I have seen other parents fight similar battles over nonessentials such as the purchase of a first bra for a flat-chested preadolescent girl. For goodness sake! If she wants it that badly, she probably needs it for social reasons. Run, don't walk, to the nearest department store and buy her a bra. The objective, as Charles and Andy Stanley wrote, is to *keep your kids on your team*. Don't throw away your friendship over behavior that has no great moral significance. There will be plenty of real issues that require you to stand like a rock. Save your big guns for those crucial confrontations.

Let me make it very clear, again, that this advice is not relevant to every teenager. The compliant kid who is doing wonderfully in school, has great friends, is disciplined in his conduct and loves his parents is not nearly so delicate. Perhaps his parents can urge him to reach even higher standards in his achievements and lifestyle. My concern, however, is for that youngster who *could* go over the falls. He is intensely angry at home and is being influenced by a carload of crummy friends. Be very careful with him. Pick and choose what is worth fighting for, and settle for something less than perfection on issues that don't really matter. *Just get him through it!*

What does this mean in practical terms? It may indicate a willingness to let his room look like a junkyard for a while. Does that surprise you? I don't like lazy, sloppy, undisciplined kids any more than you do, but given the possibilities for chaos that this angry boy or girl might precipitate, spit-shined rooms may not be all that important.

You might also compromise somewhat regarding the music you let him hear. I'm *not* condoning hard rock and heavy metal, which is saturated with explicit and illicit sex and violence today. But neither can you ask this gogo teenager to listen to your "elevator music." Perhaps a compromise can be reached. Unfortunately, the popular music of the day is the rallying cry for rebellious teenagers. If you try to deny it altogether to a strong-willed kid, you just might flip his canoe upside down. You have to ask yourself this question, "Is it worth risking everything of value to enforce a particular standard upon this son or daughter?" If the issue *is* important enough to defend at all costs, then brace yourself and make your stand. But think through those intractable matters in advance and plan your defense of them thoroughly.

The philosophy we applied with our teenagers (and you might try with yours) can be called "loosen and tighten." By this I mean we tried to loosen our grip on everything that had no lasting significance, and tighten down on everything that did. We said yes whenever we possibly could, to give support to the occasional no. And most importantly, we tried never to get too far away from our kids emotionally.

It is simply not prudent to write off a son or daughter, no matter how foolish, irritating, selfish, or insane a child may seem to be. You need to be there, not only while their canoe is bouncing precariously, but after the river runs smooth again. You have the remainder of your life to reconstruct the relationship that is now in jeopardy. Don't let anger fester for too long. Make the first move toward reconciliation. And try hard not to hassle your kids. They *hate* to be nagged. If you follow them around with one complaint after another, they are almost forced to protect themselves by appearing deaf. And finally, continue to treat them with respect, even when punishment or restrictions are necessary. Occasionally, you may even need to say, "I'm sorry!"

My father found it very difficult to say those words. I remember working with him in the backyard when I was fifteen years of age, on a day when he was particularly irritable for some reason. I probably deserved his indignation, but I thought he was being unfair. He crabbed at me for everything I did, even when I hustled. Finally, he yelled at me for something petty and that did it. He capsized my canoe. I threw down the rake and quit. Defiantly I walked across our property and down the street while my dad demanded that I come back. It was one of the few times I ever took him on like that! I meandered around town for a while, wondering what would happen to me when I finally went home. Then I strolled over to my cousin's house on the other side of town. After say. There are countless factors over which parents have no control.

The economics of the country, for example, the post-World War II money boom, with TV showing us all those wonderful things we simply couldn't live without . . . all have created a wildly acquisitive society.

And let's not forget Vietnam—the biggest mistake this country ever made. The richly deserved disgrace of losing to a small country 10,000 miles away not only infuriated a whole generation of young people, but made them anti-American and provided them with an excuse to look like bums. It also helped them get heavily involved with drugs.

But that belongs to history and now we must look to the future. We must get back to the basics and love our children enough to stop protecting them against their destructive, self-defeating behavior. Because in the end, if we allow them to destroy themselves, they will destroy us, too.[6]

[1] "Leader of the Band" by Dan Fogelberg. © 1981 APRIL MUSIC INC., and HICKORY GROVE MUSIC. All rights controlled and administered by APRIL MUSIC INC. All rights reserved. International copyright secured. Used by permission.

[2] Lewis Yablonsky, *Fathers and Sons* (New York: Simon and Schuster, Fireside Books, 1984), 134.

[3] *Los Angeles Times*, 16 June 1985. Used with permission of the author, Harold Mann, Van Nuys, California.

[4] "'Giving In' Often Seen When Kids Hit Parents," *Omaha World Herald*, 6 July 1979.

[5] *Time* Magazine, 8 June 1981.

[6] Reprinted from the November 3, 1981 issue of *Family Circle Magazine*. Copyright © 1981 THE FAMILY CIRCLE, INC.

Chapter Ten

Questions and Answers

Our discussion to this point has dealt with some heavy and troublesome issues. Other topics have been complex and difficult to explain. To help gather up the loose ends and clarify the areas we've touched superficially, we will devote this chapter to a question-and-answer format. We will hopscotch through the preceding discussions to anticipate the questions that would have been asked if I were talking directly to parents instead of writing to them.

Let's proceed, now, with the first question, which relates to the scripture misunderstood by Ann Landers.

Q. *You have said that the children of godly parents sometime go into severe rebellion and never return to the faith they were taught. I have seen that happen to some wonderful families that loved the Lord and were committed to the church. Still, it appears contradictory to Scripture. How do you interpret Proverbs 22:6, which says, "Train up a child in the way he should go, and when he is old, he will not depart from it"? Doesn't that* *verse mean, as it implies, that the children of wise and dedicated Christian parents will never be lost? Doesn't it promise that all wayward offspring will return, sooner or later, to the fold?*

A. I wish Solomon's message to us could be interpreted that confidently. I know the common understanding of the passage is to accept it as a divine guarantee, but it was not expressed in that context. Psychiatrist John White, writing in his excellent book, *Parents in Pain*, has helped me understand that the Proverbs were never intended to be absolute *promises* from God. Instead, they are *probabilities* of things which are likely to occur. Solomon, who wrote the Proverbs, was the wisest man on the earth at that time. His purpose was to convey his divinely inspired observations on the way human nature and God's universe work. A given set of circumstances can be expected to produce certain consequences. Several of these observations, including Proverbs 22:6, have been lifted out of that context and made to stand alone as promises from God. If we insist on that interpretation, then we must explain why so many other Proverbs do not inevitably prove accurate. For example:

Lazy hands make a man poor, but diligent hands bring wealth (10:4). (Have you ever met a diligent . . . but poor . . . Christian? I have.)

The blessing of the Lord brings wealth, and he adds no trouble to it (10:22).

The fear of the Lord adds length to life, but the years of the wicked are cut short (10:27). (I have watched some beautiful children die with a Christian testimony on their lips.)

No harm befalls the righteous, but the wicked have their fill of trouble (12:21).

Plans fail for lack of counsel, but with many advisers they succeed (15:22).

Gray hair is a crown of splendor; it is attained by a righteous life (16:31).

The lot is cast into the lap, but its every decision is from the Lord (16:33).

A tyrannical ruler lacks judgment, but he who hates ill-gotten gain will enjoy a long life (28:16).

We can all think of exceptions to the statements above. To repeat, they appear to represent likelihoods rather than absolutes with God's personal guarantee attached. This interpretation of Proverbs is somewhat controversial among laymen, but less so among biblical scholars. For example, the *Bible Knowledge Commentary*, prepared by the faculty of the Dallas Theological Seminary, accepts the understanding I have suggested. This commentary is recognized for its intense commitment to the literal interpretation of God's Word, yet this is what the theologians wrote:

> . . . Some parents, however, have sought to follow this directive but without this result. Their children have strayed from the godly training the parents gave them. This illustrates the nature of a "proverb." A proverb is a literary device whereby a general truth is brought to

bear on a specific situation. Many of the proverbs are not absolute guarantees for they express truths that are necessarily conditioned by prevailing circumstances. For example, verses 3–4, 9, 11, 16, and 29 do not express promises that are always binding. Though the proverbs are generally and usually true, occasional exceptions may be noted. This may be because of the self-will or deliberate disobedience of an individual who chooses to go his own way—the way of folly instead of the way of wisdom. For that he is held responsible. It is generally true, however, that most children who are brought up in Christian homes, under the influence of godly parents who teach and live God's standards, follow that training.[1]

Obviously, the humanistic concept of determinism has found its way even into the interpretation of Scripture. Those who believe Proverbs 22:6 offers a guarantee of salvation for the next generation have assumed, in essence, that a child can be programmed so thoroughly as to *determine* his course. The assignment for them is to bring him up "in the way that he should go." But think about that for a moment. Didn't the great Creator handle Adam and Eve with infinite wisdom and love? He made no mistakes in "fathering" them. They were also harbored in a perfect environment with none of the pressures we face. They had no in-law problems, no monetary needs, no frustrating employers, no television, no pornography, no alcohol or drugs, no peer pressure, and no sorrow. They had *no excuses!* Nevertheless, they ignored the explicit warning from God and stumbled into sin. If it were ever possible to avoid the ensnarement of evil, it would have occurred in that sinless world. But it didn't. God in His love gave Adam and Eve a choice between good and evil and they abused it. Will He now withhold that same freedom from your children? No. Ultimately, they will decide for themselves. That time of decision is a breathtaking moment for parents, when everything they have taught appears to be on the line. But it must come for us all.

Q. *You obviously feel very strongly about this misinterpretation of Scripture. What are its implications?*

A. I am most concerned for dedicated and sincere Christian parents whose grown sons and daughters have rebelled against God and their own families. These mothers and fathers did the best they could to raise their children properly, but they lost them anyway. That situation produces enormous guilt in itself, quite apart from scriptural understandings. Then they read in the Book of Proverbs that God has promised— absolutely guaranteed—the spiritual welfare of children whose parents trained them up properly. What are they to conclude, then, in light of continued rebellion and sin in the next generation? The message is inescapable! It must be their fault. They have damned their own kids by failing to keep their half of the bargain. They have sent their beloved children to hell by their parenting failures. This thought is so terrible for a sensitive believer that it could actually undermine his sanity.

I simply do not believe God intended for the *total* responsibility for sin in the next generation to fall on the backs of vulnerable parents. When we look at the entire Bible, we find no support for that extreme position. Cain's murder of Abel was not blamed on his parents. Joseph was a godly man and his brothers were rascals, yet their father and mother (Jacob and Rachel) were not held accountable for the differences between them. The saintly Samuel raised rebellious children, yet he was not charged with their sin. And in the New Testament, the father of the Prodigal Son was never accused of raising his adventuresome son improperly. The boy was apparently old enough to make his own headstrong decision, and his father did not stand in his way. This good man never repented of any wrongdoing—nor did he need to.

It is not my desire to let parents off the hook when they have been slovenly or uncommitted during their child-rearing years. There is at least one biblical example of God's wrath falling on a father who failed to discipline and train his sons. That incident is described in 1 Samuel 2:22–36, where Eli, the priest, permitted his sons to desecrate the temple. All three were sentenced to death by the Lord. Obviously, He takes our parenting tasks seriously and expects us to do likewise. But He does not intend for us to grovel in guilt for circumstances beyond our control!

Q. *Referring to the point you made about young married couples who overcommit themselves, you warned against trying to do too much too soon. I don't want to make that mistake, yet I do hope to get married and go on to graduate school. Would you be more specific about the advice you would offer to people like me?*

A. It seems only yesterday that I was faced with some similar questions in my own life. I was a third-year student in college, hoping to earn a Ph.D., get married, have children, buy a home, and earn a living in the next few years. Because I was young, I thought there were no limits to what I could accomplish. But then my aunt, Lela London, heard a Christian psychologist named Clyde Narramore speak one day, and he offered to spend an afternoon with any promising student who wanted to enter the field of mental health. "We need Christians in this work," he said, "and I'll help those who are interested." I called Dr. Narramore a few days later and he graciously agreed to see me. This busy man gave me two hours of his time in the living room of his home. I still remember his words thirty years later. Among other things, he warned me not to get married too quickly if I wanted to get through school and become a practicing psychologist.

He said, "A baby will come along before you know it and you will find yourself under heavy financial pressure. That will make you want to quit. You'll sit up nights caring for a sick child and then spend maybe $300 in routine medical bills. Your wife will be frustrated and you will be tempted to abandon your dreams. Don't put yourself in that straitjacket."

I accepted Dr. Narramore's advice and waited until I was twenty-four years old and had almost finished my master's degree before Shirley and I were married. We then delayed our first child for five more years until I had completed the coursework for my doctorate. It was a wise choice, although today I am listed in the *Guinness Book of Records* as "Oldest Living Father of a Teenager. " Life is a trade-off, as they say.

Though Dr. Narramore did not say so, I assure you that marital problems are almost inevitable when couples overcommit themselves during the early years. The bonding that should occur in the first decade requires time together—time that cannot be given if it is absorbed elsewhere. My advice to you is to hold onto your dreams, but take a little longer to fulfill them. Success will wait, but a happy family will not. To achieve the former and lose the latter would be an empty victory, at best.

Let me toss in this afterthought. I read an article in the *Los Angeles Times* recently about a man named J. R. Buffington. His goal in life was to produce lemons of record-breaking size from the tree in his backyard. He came up with a formula to do just that. He fertilized the tree with ashes from the fireplace, some rabbit-goat manure, a few rusty nails and plenty of water. That spring, the scrawny little tree gave birth to two gigantic lemons, one weighing over five pounds. But every other lemon on the tree was shriveled and misshapen. Mr. Buffington is still working on his formula.

Isn't that the way it is in life? Great investments in a particular endeavor tend to rob others of their potential. I'd rather have a tree covered with juicy lemons than a record-breaking but freakish crop, wouldn't you? *Balance* is the word. It is the key to successful living . . . and parenting.

Keep trying, Mr. Buffington. Have you thought about using licorice?

Q. *My three-year-old son can be counted on to behave like a brat whenever we are in the mall or in a restaurant. He seems to know I will not punish him there in front of other people. How should I handle this tactic?*

A. They tell me that a raccoon can usually kill a dog if he gets him in a lake or river. He will simply pull the hound underwater until he drowns. Most other animals would also prefer to do battle on the turf of their own choosing. It works that way with young children too. If they're going to pick a fight with Mom or Dad, they'd rather stage it in a public place, such as a supermarket or in the church foyer. They are smart enough to know that they are "safer" in front of other people. They will grab candy or speak in disrespectful ways which would never be attempted at home. Again, the most successful military generals are those who surprise the enemy in a terrain advantageous to their troops. Public facilities represent the "high ground" for a rambunctious preschooler.

You may be one of the parents who has fallen into this trap. Rather than having to discipline in public, you have inadvertently created "sanctuaries" where the old rules are not enforced. It is a certainty that your strong-willed son or daughter will behave offensively and disrespectfully in those neutral zones. There is something within the child that almost forces him to "test the limits" in situations where the resolve of adults is in question. Therefore, I recommend that you issue a stern warning *before* you enter those public arenas, making it clear that the same rules will apply. Then if he misbehaves, simply take him back to the car or around the corner and do what you would have done at home. His public behavior will improve dramatically.

Q. *I could use some advice about a minor problem we're having. Tim, my six-year-old, greatly loves to use silly names whenever he speaks to my husband and me. For example, this past week it's been "you big hot dog." Nearly every time he sees me now he says, "Hi, hot dog."*

Before that it was "dummy," then "moose" (after he studied M for moose in school).

I know it's silly and it's not a huge problem, but it gets so annoying after such a long time. He's been doing this for a year now. How can we get him to talk to us with more respect, calling us Mom or Dad, instead of hot dog and moose?

Thank you for any advice you can offer.

A. What we have here is a rather classic power game, much like those we have discussed before. And contrary to what you said, it is not so insignificant. Under other circumstances, it would be a minor matter for a child to call his parents a playful name. That is not the point here. Rather, strong-willed Tim is continuing to do something that he knows is irritating to you and your husband, yet you are unable to stop him. That is the issue. He has been using humor as a tactic of defiance for a full year. It is time for you to sit down and have a quiet little talk with young Timothy. Tell him that he is being disrespectful and that the next time he calls either you or his father a name of any kind, he will be punished. You must then be prepared to deliver on the promise, because he will continue to challenge you until it ceases to be fun. That's the way he is made. If that response never comes, his insults will probably become more pronounced, ending in adolescent nightmares. Appeasement for a strong-willed child is an invitation to warfare.

Never forget this fact: The classic strong-willed child craves power from his toddler years and even earlier. Since Mom is the nearest adult who is holding the reins, he will hack away at her until she lets him drive his own buggy. I remember a mother telling me of a confrontation with her tough-minded four-year-old daughter. The child was demanding her own way and the mother was struggling to hold her own.

"Jenny," said the mother, "you are just going to have to do what I tell you to do. I am your boss. The Lord has given me the responsibility for leading you, and that's what I intend to do!"

Jenny thought that over for a minute and then asked, "How long does it have to be that way?"

Doesn't that illustrate the point beautifully? Already at four years of age, this child was anticipating a day of *freedom* when no one could tell her what to do. There was something deep within her spirit that longed for control. Watch for the same phenomenon in your child. If he's a toughie, it will show up soon.

Q. *You have explained the dangers of power to both children and adults. But there's no great virtue in being completely powerless either, is there? What does it do to a person to be without influence or credibility in today's society?*

A. You've asked an insightful question. There is reason to be concerned about those who have been stripped of all social power in this day. The elderly, the handicapped, the poverty-stricken, the homeless, the sick, and the dying are often among that number.

My father was given a glimpse of their plight toward the end of his life. I'll never forget visiting him in the hospital for the final time after his massive heart attack. I flew in from Cincinnati that night and rushed to his bedside. I sat with him through the late hours and talked about his circumstances. He was in a contemplative mood. Dad told me that the medical staff had given him good care, but they somehow managed to convey disrespect for him. He was not angry and he didn't ask me to intercede on his behalf. That was not his point. He had simply made an observation that troubled him. He said the young doctors and nurses responded to him as though he were an old man. He was only sixty-six years of age then and was still engaged full time as a college professor. He had been a very energetic man until the pruning knife of time did its dastardly work. Now, life was rapidly winding down and he seemed to know it.

Then he said, "I have seen during these past few days what it is like to experience the absolute powerlessness of old age—where you are totally dependent on someone who does not value you as a person. I understand for the first time the disrespect that accompanies advanced age in this country. It is a frightening thing."

Millions of older people know precisely what my dad was trying to express. Being powerless is difficult even when accompanied by love and acceptance. Dependency is terrifying when surrounded by disrespect. I believe this is why Jesus came to help the down-and-outers— the wounded, lame, and sick. He touched the leper who had not been approached in years. And He told His disciples, "It is not the healthy who need a doctor, but the sick . . ." (Mark 2:17). He admonished us all, ". . . I tell you the truth, whatever you did for one of the least of these brothers of mine, you did for me" (Matthew 25:40). What incredible compassion He had for those who hurt— for the powerless people of the world. I wish I could point them all to Him. He is a friend who will stick closer than a brother.

Q. *The greatest power struggle in our home is school-work, which you mentioned, and especially homework. Our fifth grader simply will not do it! When we force him to study, he sits and stares, doodles, gets up for water, and just kills time. Furthermore, we never know for sure what his assignments are. What would you recommend?*

A. Let me offer a short discourse on school achievement, based on years of interaction with parents. I served as a teacher and I've worked as a high school counselor. Believe me, I know the agitation that mothers and fathers feel when their kids will not use the abilities God has given them. This is the situation with which they are faced: The kind of self-discipline necessary to succeed in school appears to be distributed among children on a continuum from one extreme to the other. Students at the positive end of the scale (Type I, I'll call them) are by nature rather organized individuals who care about details. They take the educational process very seriously and assume full responsibility for assignments given. They also worry about grades, or at least, they recognize their importance. To do poorly on a test would depress them for several days. They also like the challenge offered in the classroom. Parents of these children do not have to monitor their progress to keep them working. It is their way of life . . . and it is consistent with their temperament.

At the other end of the continuum are the boys and girls who do not fit in well with the structure of the classroom (Type II). If their Type I siblings emerge from school cum laude, these kids graduate "Thank You, Laude!" They are sloppy, disorganized, and flighty. They have a natural aversion to work and love to play. They can't wait

195

for success and they hurry on without it. Like bacteria that gradually become immune to antibiotics, the classic underachievers become impervious to adult pressure. They withstand a storm of parental protest every few weeks and then, when no one is looking, they slip back into apathy. They don't even hear the assignments being given in school and seem not to be embarrassed when they fail to complete them. And, you can be sure, they drive their parents to distraction.

There are several important understandings about Type I and II kids that may help parents deal with their differences. First, these characteristics are not highly correlated with intelligence. By that I mean there are bright children who are at the flighty end of the scale, and there are slow-learning individuals who are highly motivated. The primary difference between them is a matter of temperament and maturity, rather than IQ.

Second, Type II kids are not inferior to Type I. Yes, it would be wonderful if every student used the talent he possessed to best advantage. But each child is a unique individual. All don't have to fit the same mold. I know education is important today, and we want our children to go as far as they can, academically. But let's keep our goals in proper perspective. It is possible that the low achiever will outperform the academic superstar in the long run. There are countless examples of that occurring in the real world (Einstein, Edison, Roosevelt, etc.). Don't write off that disorganized, apparently lazy kid as a life-long loser. He may surprise you.

Third, you will *never* turn a Type II youngster into a Type I scholar by nagging, pushing, threatening, and punishing. It isn't in him. If you try to squeeze him into something he's not, you will only produce aggravation for yourself and anger from the child. That effort can fill a house with conflict. I have concluded that it is simply not worth the price it extracts.

On the other hand, I certainly do not recommend that children be allowed to float through life, avoiding responsibility and wasting their opportunities. My approach to the underachiever can be summarized in these suggestions: (1) He lacks the discipline to structure his life. Help him generate it. Systematize his study hours. Look over his homework to see that it is neat and complete, etc. (2) Maintain as close contact with the school as possible. The more you and your child's teacher communicate, the better. Only then can you provide the needed structure. (3) Avoid anger in the relationship. It does not help. Those parents who become most frustrated and irritated usually believe their child's irresponsibility is a deliberate thing. Usually it is not. Approach the problem as one of temperament rather than acts of defiance. (4) Having done what you can to help, accept what comes in return. Go with the flow and begin looking for other areas of success for your child. Let me say it once more: Not every individual can be squeezed into the same mold. There is room in this world for the creative "souls" who long to breathe free. I'll bet some of you as parents approached life from the same direction.

Q. *How do you feel about homework being given by schools? Do you think it is a good idea? If so, how much and how often?*

A. Having written several books on discipline and being on the record as an advocate of parental authority, my answer may surprise you: I believe homework can be destructive and counterproductive if it is not handled very carefully. I am especially concerned about large quantities of homework that are given routinely during elementary school. Little kids are asked to sit for six or more hours a day doing formal classwork. Then they take that tiring bus ride home and guess what? They're placed at a desk and told to do more assignments. For a wiry, hyperactive child or even for a fun-loving youngster, that is asking too much. Learning for them becomes an enormous bore, instead of the exciting panorama that it should be.

I remember a mother coming to see me because her son was struggling in school. "He has about five hours of homework per night," she said. "How can I make him *want* to do it?"

"Are you kidding?" I told his mother. "I wouldn't do that much homework!"

Upon investigation, I found that the private school which he attended vigorously denied giving him that many assignments. Or rather, they didn't give the *other* students that much work. They did expect the slower boys and girls to complete the assignments they didn't get done in the classroom each day plus finish the home-work. For the plodders like this youngster, that meant up to five hours of work nightly. There was no escape from books throughout their entire day. What a mistake!

Excessive homework during the elementary school years also has the potential of interfering with family life. In our home, we were trying to do many things with the limited time we had together. I wanted our kids to participate in church activities, have some family time, and still be able to kick back and waste an hour or two.

Children need opportunities for unstructured play—swinging on the swings and throwing rocks and playing with basketballs. Yet by the time that homework was done, darkness had fallen and dinnertime had arrived. Then baths were taken and off they went to bed. Something didn't feel right about that kind of pace. That's why I negotiated with our children's teachers, agreeing that they would complete no more than one hour per night of supervised homework. It was enough!

Homework also generates a considerable amount of stress for parents. Their kids either won't do the assignments or they get tired and whine about it. Tensions build and angry words fly. I'm also convinced that child abuse occurs right at that point for some children. When Shirley was teaching the second grade, one little girl came to school with both eyes black and swollen. She said her father had beaten her because she couldn't learn her spelling words. That is illegal now, but it wasn't then. The poor youngster will remember those beatings for a lifetime and will always think of herself as "stupid."

Then there are the parents who do the assignments *for* their kids just to get them over the hump. Have you ever been guilty of that illegality? Shame on you! More specifically, have you ever worked for two weeks on a fifth-grade geography project for your nonacademic eleven-year-old—and then learned later that you got a C on it?! That's the ultimate humiliation.

In short, I believe homework in elementary school should be extremely limited. It is appropriate for learning multiplication tables, spelling words, and test review. It is also helpful in training kids to remember assignments, bring books home, and complete them as required. But to load them down night after night with monotonous bookwork is to invite educational burnout.

In junior high classes, perhaps an hour of homework per night should be the maximum. In high school, those students who are preparing for college may handle more work. Even then, however, the load should be reasonable. Education is a vitally important part of our children's lives, but it is only *one* part. Balance between these competing objectives is the key word.

Q. *May I go back to the story of the undisciplined toddler on the airplane? You described her as being unruly and unwilling to be buckled in her seat. How would you have handled that situation?*

A. Well, I think I mentioned that a few sharp slaps on the legs would have curtailed her temper tantrum and given control back to the mother. On the other hand, the crisis need never have developed. The mother should have anticipated that situation and brought some sugarless mints and a few interesting toys or playthings. That would have been so easy to do. Instead, mom and daughter were like two freight trains coming together on the same track. A violent collision was inevitable. I just happened to be there to witness the crash.

Q. *You've made a big deal over the issue of newborns and whether or not they come into the world with complex temperaments or as "blank slates." When all is said and done, what difference does it make? Children are children, and we take them as we find them. Why does it matter whether they began with "something" or with "nothing"?*

A. It is easy to see how you could assume that this

issue is of academic interest only, with no practical application. Nothing could be further from the truth. These contrasting ways of perceiving children have far-reaching implications and will influence parenting techniques throughout the developmental years. Let me explain.

The "blank slate" theory holds that children are born neutral but with a penchant for "good." Their natural tendency is to love, give, work, cooperate, and learn. The failure of the individual to behave in these positive ways does not result from any internal flaw, but rather from a corrupt and misguided society. Bad *experiences* are responsible for bad behavior. Therefore, it is the task of parents to provide a loving environment and then stay out of the way. Natural goodness will flow from it. As long as major mistakes are avoided, there will be no negative stimuli to distort or warp the developing individual. Rebellion and disobedience do not emanate from love. Thus, parental discipline is of lesser significance because there is no inner nature to be confronted.

This is the humanistic perspective on childish nature. Millions of Americans and Canadians, the majority no doubt, believe it to be true. Most psychologists have also accepted and taught it throughout the twentieth century. There is only one thing wrong with the concept: It is entirely inaccurate.

It is impossible to understand human nature without consulting the "Owners Manual." Only the Creator of children can tell us how He made them, and He has done that in Scripture. It teaches that we are born in sin, having inherited a disobedient nature from Adam. King David said, ". . . in sin did my mother *conceive* me" (Psalm

51:5), meaning that this tendency to do wrong was transmitted genetically. It has infected every person who ever lived. "For *all* have sinned and come short of the glory of God" (Romans 3:23). Therefore, with or without bad experiences, a child is naturally inclined toward rebellion, selfishness, dishonesty, aggression, exploitation, and greed. He does not have to be taught these behaviors. They are inevitable expressions of his humanness.

Although this perspective on man is mocked in the secular world today, abundant evidence attests to its accuracy. How else do we explain the pugnacious and perverse nature of every society on earth? Bloody warfare has been the centerpiece of world history for more than 5,000 years. People of every race and creed around the globe have tried to rape, plunder, burn, blast, and kill each other century after century. Peace was merely a momentary pause when they stopped to reload! Plato said more than 2,350 years ago, "Only dead men have seen an end to war." He was right, at least until the Prince of Peace comes.

Furthermore, in the midst of these warring nations we find a depressing incidence of murder, drug abuse, child molestation, prostitution, adultery, homosexuality, and dishonesty. How do we explain this pervasive evil in a world of people who are naturally inclined toward good? Have they really drifted into these antisocial behaviors despite their inborn tendencies? If so, surely *one* society in all the world has been able to preserve the goodness with which children are born. Where is it? Does such a place exist? No, even though some societies are more moral than others, none reflects the harmony which might be expected from the "blank slate" theorists. Why not? Because the premise is wrong.

What, then, does this biblical understanding mean for parents? Are they to look on their babies as guilty before they have done wrong? Of course not. Children are not responsible for their sins until they reach an age of accountability—and that time frame is known best to God. On the other hand, parents would be wise to anticipate and deal with rebellious behavior when it occurs. And it *will* occur, probably by the eighteenth month or before. Anyone who has watched a toddler throw a violent temper tantrum when he doesn't get his way must be hard-pressed to explain how that particular "blank slate" got so mixed up! Did his mother or father model the tantrum for him, falling on the floor, slobbering, kicking, crying, and screaming? I would hope not. Either way, the kid needs no demonstration. Rebellion comes naturally to him.

Parents can, and must, train, shape, mold, correct, guide, punish, reward, instruct, warn, teach, and love their kids during the formative years. Their purpose is to control that inner nature and keep it from tyrannizing the entire family. Ultimately, however, only Jesus Christ can cleanse it and make it "wholly acceptable" to the Master.

You know what? I believe I've preached a sermon. And I'm not even a minister.

Q. *Generally speaking, what kind of discipline do you use with a teenager who is habitually miserable to live with?*

A. In addition to what I've already written on this subject, let me offer this thought: The general rule is to use action—not anger—to reach an understanding. Anytime you can get teenagers to do what is necessary without becoming furious at them, you are ahead of the game. Let me provide a few examples of how this might be accomplished.

(1) In Russia, I'm told that teenagers who are convicted of using drugs are denied driver's licenses for years. It is a very effective approach.

(2) When my daughter was a teenager, she used to slip into my bathroom and steal my razor, my shaving cream, my toothpaste, or my comb. Of course, she never brought them back. Then after she had gone to school, I would discover the utensils missing. There I was with wet hair or "fuzzy" teeth, trying to locate the confiscated item in *her* bathroom. It was no big deal, but it was irritating at the time. Can you identify?

I asked Danae a dozen times not to do this, but to no avail. Thus, the phantom struck without warning one cold morning. I hid everything she needed to put on her "face," and then left for the office. My wife told me she had never heard such wails and moans as were uttered that day. Our daughter plunged desperately through bathroom drawers looking for her toothbrush, comb, and hair dryer. The problem has never resurfaced.

(3) A family living in a house with a small hot-water tank was continually frustrated by their teenager's endless showers. Screaming at him did no good. Once he was locked behind the bathroom door, he stayed in the steamy stall until the last drop of warm water had been drained. Solution? In midstream, Dad stopped the flow of hot water by turning a valve at the tank. Cold water suddenly poured from the nozzle. Junior popped out of the shower in seconds.

(4) A single mother couldn't get her daughter out of

bed in the morning until she announced a new policy: The hot water would be shut off promptly at 6:30 A.M. The girl could either get up on time or bathe in ice water. Another mother had trouble getting her eight-year-old out of bed each morning. She then began pouring bowls of frozen marbles under the covers with him each morning. He arose quite quickly.

(5) Instead of standing in the parking lot and screaming at students who drive too fast, school officials now put huge bumps in the road that jar the teeth of those who ignore them. It does the job quite nicely.

(6) You as the parent have the car that a teenager needs, the money that he covets, and the authority to grant or withhold privileges. If push comes to shove, these chips can be exchanged for commitments to live responsibly, share the workload at home, and stay off little brother's back. This bargaining process works for younger kids too. I like the "one to one" trade-off for television viewing time. It permits a child to watch one minute of television for every minute spent reading. The possibilities are endless.

Q. *Would you ever, under any circumstances, permit a son or daughter to bring a roomie of the opposite sex into your home to live?*

A. No. It would be dishonoring to God and a violation of the moral principles on which Shirley and I have staked our lives. I will bend for my kids, but never that far.

Q. *Are there times when good, loving parents don't like their own kids very much?*

A. Yes, just as there are times in a good marriage

205

when husbands and wives don't like each other for a while. What you should do in both situations is hang tough. Look for ways to make the relationship better, but never give up your commitment to one another. That is especially true during the teen years, when the person we see will be *very* different in a few years. Wait patiently for him to grow up. You'll be glad you did.

NOTE: The following item was originally published in my earlier book, *Straight Talk to Men and Their Wives*, but it is also being included here because of its relevancy to the topic. Someone needs to read this message! Is it you?

Q. *My wife and I are new Christians, and we now realize that we raised our kids by the wrong principles. They're grown now, but we continue to worry about the past and we feel great regret for our failures as parents. Is there anything we can do at this late date?*

A. Let me deal, first, with the awful guilt you are obviously carrying. There's hardly a parent alive who does not have some regrets and painful memories of failures as a mother or a father. Children are infinitely complex as I've indicated, and we cannot be perfect parents any more than we can be perfect human beings. The pressures of living are stressful and we get tired and irritated; we are influenced by our physical bodies and our emotions, which sometimes prevent us from saying the right things and being the model we should be. We don't always handle our children as unemotionally as we wish we had, and it's very common to look back a year or two later and see how wrong we were in the way we approached a problem.

All of us experience these failures! That's why each of us should get alone with the Creator of parents and children and say: "Lord, You know my inadequacies. You know my weaknesses, not only in parenting, but in every area of my life. I did the best I could, but it wasn't good enough. As You broke the fishes and the loaves to feed the five thousand, now take my meager effort and use it to bless my family. Make up for the things I did wrong. Satisfy the needs that I have not satisfied. Wrap Your great arms around my children, and draw them close to You. And be there when they stand at the great cross-roads between right and wrong. All I can give is my best, and I've done that. Therefore, I submit to You my children and myself and the job I did as a parent. The outcome now belongs to You."

I know God will honor that prayer, even for parents whose job is finished. The Lord does not want you to suffer from guilt over events you can no longer influence. The past is the past. Let it die, never to be resurrected. Give the situation to God, once and for all time. I think you'll be surprised to learn that you're no longer alone! ". . . forgetting what is behind and straining toward what is ahead, I press on toward the goal to win the prize for which God has called me heavenward in Christ Jesus" (Philippians 3:13–14) .

For the benefit of the discouraged mother of a strong-willed toddler who feels like she's about to lose her mind, I am herewith providing a portion of two letters sent to me a few years ago. The first was written by an exasperated mother who felt she did not get the help she needed in my book, *The Strong-Willed Child*. The second letter came from the same woman, five years later. The first letter, written October 14, 1978:

PARENTING ISN'T FOR COWARDS

Dear Dr. Dobson,

After purchasing your new book I must tell you I was disappointed. The beginning was encouraging, but then the rest was devoted to general child-rearing techniques. I thought the entire book was written about the strong-willed child. Are you sure you know what one is? Nearly every child is strong-willed, but not every child is *strong-willed!*

Our third (and last) daughter is *strong-willed!* She is twenty-one months old now, and there have been times when I thought she must be abnormal. If she had been my firstborn child there would have been no more in this family. She had colic day and night for six months, then we just quit calling it that. She was simply unhappy all the time. She began walking at eight months and she became a merciless bully with her sisters. She pulled hair, bit, hit, pinched, and pushed with all her might. She yanked out a handful of her sister's long black hair.

NOTE: This mother went on to describe the characteristics of her tyrannical daughter which I have heard thousands of times. She then closed, advising me to give greater emphasis to the importance of corporal punishment for this kind of youngster. I wrote her a cordial letter in reply and told her I understood her frustration. Five years later, she wrote to me again, as follows:

February 2, 1983

Dear Dr. Dobson,

This letter is long overdue, but, thank you! Thank you for a caring reply to what was probably not a very nice letter from a discouraged mom. Thank you for your positive remarks, the first I had had in a long time.

Perhaps you would be interested in an update on our Sally Ann. Back when I wrote to you, she was probably a perfect "10" when it came to strong-willedness. "Difficult" hardly scratches the surface of descriptive words for her babyhood. As Christian parents, we tried every scriptural method we could find for dealing with her. I had decided she was abnormal. Something so innocent as offering her her morning juice (which she loved) in the wrong glass threw her into thirty minutes of tantrums—and this was before she could really talk!

Family dinners were a nightmare. Before she turned two, Sally Ann would regularly brutalize her older sisters, ages four, eight, and twelve, even having the twelve-year-old in tears many times. A spanking from me did not deter her in the least. Finally, in prayer one day the Lord plainly showed me that her sisters must be allowed to retaliate, something I was strictly against (and still am!). However, in this case, all I can say is that it worked. I carefully and clearly told my four girls (little Sally Ann in my lap) what they were to do the next time they were attacked by their littlest sister: they were to give her a good smack on the top of her chubby little leg, next to her diaper. Sally got the point: within two days the attacks ceased.

Disciplining our youngest was never easy, but with God's help, we persevered. When she had to be spanked, we could expect up to an hour of tantrums. It would have been so easy to give in and ignore the misbehavior, but I am convinced that, without it, our Sally would have become at best a holy terror, and at worst, mentally ill. Tell your listeners that discipline *does* pay off, when administered according to the Word of God.

Sally today is a precious six-year-old and a joy to her family. She is still rather strong-willed, but it is well within normal limits now! She is very bright and has a gentle, creative, and sympathetic nature unusual in one so young. I know the Lord has great plans for her. She has already asked Jesus into her life and knows how to call upon Him when she has a need (like fear from a nightmare, etc.).

In conclusion, though I still don't think you went far enough in your book, loving discipline certainly is the key. With perseverance!

Thank you and may God's continued blessing be upon you and your household and your ministry, through Jesus Christ our Lord.

In His love,
Mrs. W W

FINAL NOTE: Thank you, too, Mrs. W. It was a special treat to hear from you again. You're on the right track with Sally Ann. Discipline with love was God's idea. Oh, and by the way, *this* book was written for you. Did I get it said this time?

James Dobson

---

[1] John Walvoord and Roy Zuck, eds., *Bible Knowledge Commentary, Old Testament* (Wheaton, Ill: Victor Books, 1985), 953.

Chapter Eleven

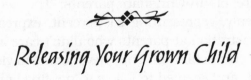

Releasing Your Grown Child

*W*e come now to the final task assigned to mothers and fathers . . . that of releasing grown children and launching them into the world of adulthood. It is also one of the most difficult. Several years ago, we explored this topic by conducting another informal poll of the Focus on the Family radio listeners. I asked them to react to this question: "What are the greatest problems you face in dealing with your parents or in-laws, and how will you relate differently to your grown children than your parents have to you?" An avalanche of mail flooded my offices in the next few days, eventually totaling more than twenty-six hundred detailed replies.

We read every letter and catalogued the responses according to broad themes. As is customary in such inquiries, the results surprised our entire staff. We fully expected in-law complaints to represent the most common category of concerns. Instead, it ranked fifth in frequency, representing only 10 percent of the letters we received. The fourth most commonly mentioned problem, at 11 percent, related to sickness, dependency, senility, and other medical problems in the older generation. In third place, at 19 percent, was general concern for the spiritual welfare of un-Christian parents. The second most common reply, representing 21 percent, expressed irritation and frustration at parents who didn't care about their children or grandchildren. They never came to visit, wouldn't baby-sit, and seemed to follow a "me-first" philosophy.

That brings us to the top of the hit parade of problems between adults and their parents. May I have the envelope please? (Drum roll in background.) And the winner is, the inability or unwillingness of parents to release their grown children and permit them to live their own lives. An incredible 44 percent of the letters received made reference to this failure of older adults to let go. It was as though some of the writers had been waiting for years for that precise question to be asked. Here are a few of their comments:

1. "Mother felt my leaving home was an insult to her. She couldn't let go, couldn't realize I needed to become an independent person, couldn't understand that I no longer needed her physical help, although I did need her as a person. Quite unintentionally she retarded my growing up by 35 years."

2. "One of the greatest problems is to have my parents see me as an adult, not as a child who doesn't know the best way to do things. As a child, I played a specific role in my family. Now as an adult, I wish to change my role, but they will not allow it."

3. "Our parents never seemed able to grasp the reality of the fact that we had grown from dependent children, to capable, responsible adults. They did not recognize or appreciate our abilities, responsibilities, or contributions to the outside world."

4. "I am 54 years old but when I visit my mother I am still not allowed to do certain things such as peel carrots, etc. because I do not do them correctly. Our relationship is still child-parent. I am still regularly corrected, criticized, put-down, and constantly reminded of what terrible things I did 50 years ago. Now we are not talking about major criminal acts, just normal childish disobedience during the preschool years. I was the youngest of five and the only daughter and I still hear, 'I would rather have raised another four boys than one daughter.' Pray for me, please. I need Jesus to help me forgive and forget."

We received literally hundreds of letters expressing this general concern. The writers wanted desperately to be free, to be granted adult status, and especially, to be respected by their parents. At the same time, they were saying to them, "I still love you. I still need you. I still want you as my friend. But I no longer need you as the authority in my life."

I remember going through a similar era in my own life. My parents handled me wisely in those years and it was rare to have them stumble into common parental mistakes. However, we had been a very close-knit family, and it was difficult for my mother to shift gears when I graduated from high school. During that summer, I traveled fifteen hundred miles from home and entered a college in California. I will never forget the exhilarating feeling of freedom that swept over me that fall. It was not that I wanted to do anything evil or previously forbidden. It was simply that I felt accountable for my own life and did not have to explain my actions to my parents. It was like a fresh, cool breeze on a spring morning. Young adults who have not been properly trained for that moment sometimes go berserk in the absence of authority, but I did not. I did, however, quickly become addicted to that freedom and was not inclined to give it up.

The following December, my parents and I met for Christmas vacation at the home of some relatives. Suddenly, I found myself in conflict with my mom. She was responding as she had six months earlier when I was still in high school. By then, I had journeyed far down the path toward adulthood. She was asking me what time I would be coming in at night, and urging me to drive the car safely, and watching what I ate. No offense was intended, mind you. My mother had just failed to notice that I had changed and she needed to get with the new program, herself.

Finally, there was a brief flurry of words between us and I left the house in a huff. A friend picked me up and I talked about my feelings as we rode in the car. "Darn it, Bill!" I said. "I don't *need* a mother anymore!"

Then a wave of guilt swept over me, as though I had said, "I don't love my mother anymore." I meant no such thing. What I was feeling was the desire to be friends with my parents instead of accepting a line of authority from them. My wish was granted by my mom and dad very quickly thereafter.

Most parents in our society do not take the hint so easily. I'm convinced that mothers and fathers in North America are among the very best in the world. We care passionately about our kids and would do anything to meet their needs. But we are among the worst when it comes to letting go of our grown sons and daughters. In fact those two characteristics are linked. The same commitment that leads us to do so well when the children are small (dedication, love, concern, involvement), also causes us to hold on too tightly when they are growing up. I will admit to my own difficulties in this area. I understood the importance of turning loose before our kids were born. I wrote extensively on the subject when they were still young. I prepared a film series in which all the right principles were expressed. But when it came time to open my hand and let the birds fly, I struggled mightily!

Why? Well, fear played a role in my reluctance. We live in Los Angeles where weird things are done by strange people every day of the year. For example, our daughter was held at gunpoint on the campus of the University of Southern California late one night. Her assailant admonished Danae not to move or make a noise. She figured her chances of survival were better by defying him right then than by cooperating. She fled. The man did not shoot at her, thank God. Who knows what he had in mind for her?

A few days later, my son was walking his bicycle across a busy road near our home when a man in a sports car came around the curve at high speed. Skid marks later showed he was traveling in excess of eighty miles per hour. Ryan saw that he was going to be hit, and he jumped over the handlebars and attempted to crawl to safety. The car was fishtailing wildly and careening toward our son. It came to a stop just inches from his head, and then the driver sped off without getting out. Perhaps he was on PCP or cocaine. Thousands of addicts live here in Los Angeles, and innocent people are victimized by them every day.

Such near-misses make me want to gather my children around me and never let them experience risk again. Of course, that is impossible and would be unwise even if they submitted to it. Life itself is a risk, and parents must let their kids face reasonable jeopardy on their own. Nevertheless, when Danae or Ryan leave in the car, I'm still tempted to say, "Be sure to keep the shiny side up and the rubber side down!"

What are *your* reasons for restricting the freedom of your grown or nearly grown children? In some cases, if we're honest, we need them too much to let them go. They have become an extension of ourselves, and our egos are inextricably linked to theirs. Therefore, we not only seek to hold them to us, but we manipulate them to maintain our control. As described in chapter 7, we use guilt, bribery, threats, intimidation, fear, and anger to restrict their freedom. And sadly, when we win at this game, we *and* our offspring are destined to lose.

Many of the letters we received in response to our poll were written by young adults who had not yet broken free. Some stories they told were almost hard to believe in a culture which legally emancipates its children at such a young age. Consider this excerpt from a young lady with very possessive parents:

> I'm 23 and the eldest of 3 children. My parents are still overprotective. They won't let go. I have a career and a very stable job but they will not allow me to move out on my own. They still try to discipline me with a spanking using a belt and hold me to a 10:00 P.M. curfew. Even if it is a church activity, I must be home by 10:00 P.M. If it's out of town or impossible for me to be home by that time, I'm not allowed to go. I have high Christian moral standards and they trust me, but they are just overprotective.

Can you imagine these parents spanking this twenty-three-year-old woman for her minor infractions and disobediences? Though I do not know the girl or her parents, it would appear that they have a classic dependency problem occurring commonly with a very compliant child. No self-respecting strong-willed individual would tolerate such dominance and disrespect. A compliant girl might, while harboring deep resentment all the while.

In a sense, this twenty-three-year-old is equally responsible for her lack of freedom. She has permitted her parents to treat her like a child. First Corinthians 13:11 says, "When I was a child, I talked like a child, I thought like a child, I reasoned like a child. When I became a man, I put childish ways behind me." What could be more childish than for a woman in her twenties to yield to a physical thrashing for arriving home after 10:00 P.M.? Of course, I believe young adults should continue to listen to the accumulated wisdom of their parents and to treat them with respect. However, the relationship must change when adolescence is over. And if the parents will not or cannot make that transformation, the son or daughter is justified in respectfully insisting that it happen. For the very compliant child, that tearing loose is extremely difficult to accomplish!

Parents who refuse to let go often force their sons or daughters to choose between two bad alternatives. The first is to accept their domination and manipulation. That is precisely what the twenty-three-year-old girl had done. Instinctively, she knew her parents were wrong, but she lacked the courage to tell them so. Thus, she remained under their authoritative umbrella for a couple of years too long. She was like an unborn baby in the tenth or eleventh month of pregnancy. Granted, the womb was safe and warm, but she could grow no more until she got past the pain and indignities of childbirth. She was overdue for "delivery" into the opportunities and responsibilities of adulthood.

To repeat our now familiar theme, it is the very compliant child who often yields to the tyranny of intimidation. Some remain closeted there for forty years or more. Even if they marry, their parents will not grant emancipation without a struggle, setting the stage for lifelong in-law problems.

The other alternative is to respond like a mountainous volcano which blows its top. Hot lava descends on everything in its path. Great anger and resentment characterize the parent-child relationship for years, leaving scars and wounds on both generations. The strong-willed individual typically chooses this response to parental domination. He isn't about to let anyone hem him in, but in the process of breaking free, he loses the support and fellowship of the family he needs.

The legendary Beatles rock group often sang about

drug usage and revolution, among other antiestablishment themes. But occasionally, their music was devastatingly incisive. One of their best renditions was recorded in 1967. It went to the heart of this matter of breaking free. The lyrics described a young woman whose parents had held on too long, forcing her to steal away in the early morning hours. Perhaps you will feel the pain of her confused parents as you read the words to *She's Leaving Home.*

Wedn'sday morning at five o'clock as the day begins
Silently closing her bedroom door
Leaving the note that she hoped would say more
She goes downstairs to the kitchen clutching
    her handkerchief
Quietly turning the backdoor key
Stepping outside, she is free.
She (We gave her most of our lives)
Is leaving (Sacrificed most of our lives)
Home (We gave her everything money could buy).
She's leaving home after living alone
    for so many years. Bye-Bye.

Father snores as his wife gets into her dressing gown
Picks up the letter that's lying there
Standing alone at the top of the stairs
She breaks down and cries to her husband,
"Daddy, our baby's gone!"
Why would she treat us so thoughtlessly?
How could she do this to me?
She (We never thought of ourselves)
Is leaving (Never a thought for ourselves)
Home (We struggled hard all our lives to get by).

PARENTING ISN'T FOR COWARDS

> She's leaving home after living alone
>> for so many years. Bye-Bye.
>
> Friday morning at nine o'clock she is far away
> Waiting to keep the appointment she made
> Meeting a man from the motor trade
> She (What did we do that was wrong?)
> Is having (We didn't know it was wrong)
> Fun (Fun is the one thing that money can't buy).
> Something inside that was always denied
>> for so many years. Bye-Bye.
> She's leaving home. Bye-Bye.[1]

There must be a better way to launch a postadolescent son or daughter, and of course there is. It is the responsibility of parents to release the grip and set the fledgling adult free to make it on his own. But alas, independence sometimes fails not because parents have withheld it, but because immature sons and daughters refuse to accept it. They have no intention of growing up. Why should they? The nest is too comfortable at home. Food is prepared, temperature is regulated, clothes are laundered, and all bills are paid. There is no incentive to face the cold world of reality, and they are determined not to budge. Some even refuse to work. They keep hours like hamsters, staying up (and out) all night and then sleeping half the day. They sit around the house listening to electronic music and waiting for a dish to rattle in the kitchen. Three months worth of dirty underwear and who knows what else are stuffed under the bed. Life is a lark, albeit a boring one. Even when they do move away for a time, they inevitably run out of money and come dragging home at mealtime. Their parents remind me of a man with a new boomerang. He would have made it fine except he went crazy trying to throw the old one away.

I received a letter from the mother of one of these perpetual freeloaders a few years ago. Let me share what she asked and how I replied:

Q. *We have a twenty-one-year-old who is still living at home. He does not want to come under our authority and he breaks all the rules we have set up as minimum standards of behavior. He plays his stereo so loudly that it drives me crazy, and he comes in every night after 1 A.M. I know he needs his freedom, but I worry about our younger children who are trying to get away with the same things their big brother does. How would you balance the rights and privileges of this young adult with our needs as a family?*

A. It is very difficult for a strong-willed twenty-one year-old to continue living at home, and it will become even more unsettling with every year that passes. The demand for independence and freedom in such cases is almost always in conflict with the parents expectations and wishes. Your son's unwillingness to respect your reasonable requests is a surefire indication that he needs to face life on his own. Also, the bad modeling he is providing for your younger siblings is a serious matter. I think it is time to help him pack. At the very least, he should be made to understand that his continued residency at home is conditional. Either live with the rules— or live with the YMCA.

I know it's difficult to dislodge a homebound son or daughter. They are like furry puppies who hang around the back door waiting for a warm saucer of milk. How can you yell "Shoo!" at someone so lost and needy? But to let them stay year after year, especially if they are pursuing no career goals or if they are disrespectful at home, is to cultivate irresponsibility and dependency. That is not love, even though it may feel like it.

We are agreed, then, that independence and freedom must be granted to those who have passed through the far side of adolescence. But how is that accomplished? The Amish have a unique approach to it. Their children are kept under the absolute authority of their parents throughout childhood. Very strict discipline and harsh standards of behavior are imposed from infancy. When they turn sixteen years of age, however, they enter a period called "Rumspringa." Suddenly, all restrictions are lifted. They are free to drink, smoke, date, marry, or behave in ways that horrify their parents. Some do just that. But most don't. They are even granted the right to leave the Amish community if they choose. But if they stay, it must be in accordance with the rules of convention. The majority accept the heritage of their forefathers, not because they must, but because they wish to.

Although I admire the Amish and many of their approaches to child-rearing, I believe the Rumspringa concept is too precipitous. To take a child overnight from total domination to absolute freedom is an invitation to anarchy. Perhaps it works in the controlled environment of Amish country, but it is usually disastrous for the rest of us. I've seen families emulate this "instant adulthood" idea, lifting parental governance overnight. The result has been similar to what occurred in African colonies when European leadership was suddenly withdrawn.

Bloody revolutions were often fought in the heady spirit of freedom.

It is better, I believe, to begin releasing your children during the preschool years, granting independence that is consistent with their age and maturity. When a child can tie his shoes, let him—yes, require him—to do it. When he can choose his own clothes within reason, let him make his own selection. When he can walk safely to school, allow him the privilege. Each year, more *responsibility* and *freedom* (they are companions) are given to the child so that the final release in early adulthood is merely the final relaxation of authority. That is the theory, at least. Pulling it off is sometimes quite difficult.

However you go about transferring the reins of authority—the rudiments of power—to your children, the task should be completed by twenty and no later than twenty-two years of age. To hold on longer is to invite revolution.

---

[1] "She's Leaving Home" by John Lennon and Paul McCartney. © 1967 NORTHERN SONGS LIMITED. All rights in the USA , CANADA, MEXICO, and the PHILIPPINES controlled and administered by BLACKWOOD MUSIC INC., under license from ATV music (MACLEN). All rights reserved. International copyright secured. Used by permission.

Chapter Twelve

A Final Thought

Perhaps we can summarize our discussion of parenthood and its tougher dimensions by answering a question posed to me recently by a puzzled mother. It went something like this:

> Tell me why it is that some kids with every advantage and opportunity seem to turn out bad, while others raised in terrible homes become pillars in the community? I know one young man, for example, who grew up in squalid circumstances, yet he is such a fine person today. How did his parents manage to raise such a responsible son when they didn't even seem to care?

Curious cases of this type are not so uncommon around us and they validate the theme of this book. As we have seen, environmental influences in themselves will not account for the behavior we observe in our fellowman. There is something else there—something from within—that also operates to make us who we are. Some behavior is caused and some plainly isn't.

Just last month, for example, I had dinner with two parents who have unofficially "adopted" a thirteen-year-old boy. This youngster followed their son home one afternoon, and then asked if he could spend the night. As it turned out, he stayed with them for almost a week without so much as a phone call coming from his mother. It was later learned that she works sixteen hours a day and has no interest in her son. Her alcoholic husband divorced her several years ago and left town without a trace. The boy had been abused, unloved, and ignored through much of his life.

Given this background, what kind of kid do you think he is today—a druggie? A foul-mouthed delinquent? A lazy, insolent bum? No. He is polite to adults; he is a hard worker; he makes good grades in school and he enjoys helping around the house. This boy is like a lost puppy who desperately wants a good home. He has begged the family to adopt him officially so he could have a real father and a loving mother. His own mom couldn't care less.

How is it that this teenager could be so well-disciplined and polished despite his lack of training? I don't know. It is simply within him. He reminds me of my wonderful friend, David Hernandez. David and his parents came to America illegally from Mexico more than forty years ago and nearly starved to death before they found work. They eventually survived by helping to harvest the potato crop throughout the state of California. During this era, David lived under trees or in the open fields. His father made a stove out of an oil drum half-filled with dirt. The open campfire was their home.

David never had a roof over his head until his parents

finally moved into an abandoned chicken coop. His mother covered the boarded walls with cheap wallpaper and David thought they were living in luxury. Then one day, the city of San Jose condemned the area and David's "house" was torn down. He couldn't understand why the community would destroy so fine a place.

Given this beginning, how can we explain the man that Dave Hernandez became? He graduated near the top of his class in high school and was granted a scholarship to college. Again, he earned high marks and four years later entered Loma Linda University School of Medicine. Once more, he scored in the top 10 percent of his class and continued in a residency in obstetrics and gynecology. Eventually, he served as a professor of OB/GYN at both Loma Linda University and the University of Southern California Medical Schools. Then at the peak of his career, his life began to unravel.

I'll never forget the day Dr. Hernandez called me on the telephone. He had just been released from hospital care following a battery of laboratory tests. The diagnosis? Sclerosing cholangitis, a liver disorder that is invariably fatal. We lost this fine husband, father, and friend six years later at the age of forty-three. I loved him like a brother and I still miss him today.

Again, I ask, how could such discipline and genius come from these infertile circumstances? Who would have thought that this deprived Mexican boy sitting out there in the dirt would someday become one the most loved and respected surgeons of his era? Where did the motivation originate? From what bubbling spring did his ambition and thirst for knowledge flow? He had no books, took no educational trips, knew no scholars. Yet he reached for the sky. Why did it happen to David Hernandez and not the youngster with every advantage and opportunity? Why have so many children of prominent and loving parents grown up in ideal circumstances, only to reject it all for the streets of San Francisco or New York? Good answers are simply not available. It apparently comes down to this: God chooses to use some individuals in unique ways. Beyond that mysterious relationship, we must simply conclude that some kids seem born to make it and others are determined to fail. Someone reminded me recently that the same boiling water that softens the carrot also hardens the egg. Likewise, some individuals react positively to certain circumstances and others negatively. We don't know why.

One thing is clear to me: Behavioral scientists have been far too simplistic in their explanation of human behavior. We are more than the aggregate of our experiences. We are more than the quality of our nutrition. We are more than our genetic heritage. We are more than our biochemistry. And certainly, we are more than our parents' influence. God has created us as unique individuals, capable of independent and rational thought that is not attributable to *any* source. That is what makes the task of parenting so challenging and rewarding. Just when you think you have your kids figured out, you had better brace yourself! Something new is coming your way.

I've spent more than half my life studying children, yet my own kids continue to surprise and fascinate me. I remember calling home some years ago from a city in Georgia where I had traveled for a speaking engagement.

Danae, who was then thirteen years of age, picked up the phone and we had a warm father-daughter chat. Then she said, "Oh, by the way, Dad, I'm going to be running in a track meet next Saturday."

"Really?" I said. "What distance have you chosen?"

"The 880," she replied.

I gasped. "Danae, that is a very grueling race. Do you know how far 880 yards is?"

"Yes," she said. "It's a half-mile."

"Have you ever run that far before?" I asked.

She said that she hadn't, even in practice. I continued to probe for information and learned that nine schools would be competing in the meet, which was only three days away. My daughter intended to compete against a field of other runners who presumably had been training for weeks. I was concerned.

"Danae," I said, "you've made a big mistake. You're about to embarrass yourself and I want you to think it over. You should go to your coach and ask to run a shorter race. At that speed 880 yards will kill you!"

"No, Dad," she said with determination. "No one else signed up for the 880 and I want to run it."

"Okay," I replied, "but you're doing it against my better judgment."

I thought about that beloved kid the rest of the week and wondered what humiliation was in store for her. I called again on Saturday afternoon.

"Guess what, Dad!" Danae said cheerfully. "I won the race today!" She had indeed finished in first place, several yards ahead of her nearest competitor. The following year, also without training, she won the same race by fifty yards and set a school record that may still be standing.

Wow! I said to myself. *The kid has talent. She'll be a great runner someday.* Wrong again. She ran and won two races in the ninth grade, came in second in the next, and then lost interest in track. End of story.

So much for fatherly wisdom in all its glory.

Obviously, I am deeply respectful of the human personality and the stunning complexity of even our youngest members. In a sense, this entire book has been a testimony to them and to those of you as parents who are dedicated to their care. I admire each of you greatly and I hope we have been of assistance in fulfilling your awesome responsibility. Now in these concluding paragraphs, I would like to express two or three final thoughts directly to the mothers and fathers of very rebellious kids. I am especially concerned about you.

First, I know your task is difficult and there are times when you feel like throwing in the towel. But you must remain steady. Someday, you will look back on this difficult period of conflict and be thankful that you stayed on course—that you continued to do what was right for those children whom God loaned to you for a season. This era will pass so quickly, and the present stresses will seem insignificant and remote. What will matter to you then will be the loving relationships you built with your family, even when other parents ran away or buried themselves in work. You will also have the knowledge of a job well done in the eyes of the Creator Himself.

Therefore, I hope you will resist the temptation to feel cheated or deprived because of the difficult temperament of your son or daughter. You are certainly not alone. In an earlier survey of 3,000 parents, we found that 85 percent of families had at least one strong-willed child. So, you are not an exception or the butt of some cruel cosmic joke. This is parenthood. This is human nature. Most of us who have raised two or more kids have gone through some of the same stresses you are experiencing. We survived, and you will too. You can handle the assignment.

Let me review the concepts we have considered in our meandering discussion of children:

1. You are not to blame for the temperament with which your child was born. He is simply a tough kid to handle and your task is to rise to the challenge.

2. He is in greater danger because of his inclination to test the limits and scale the walls. Your utmost diligence and wisdom will be required to deal with him.

3. If you fail to understand his lust for power and independence, you can exhaust your resources and bog down in guilt. It will benefit no one.

4. If it is not already too late, by all means, take charge of your babies. Hold tightly to the reins of authority in the early days, and build an attitude of respect during your brief window of opportunity. You will need every ounce of "awe" you can get during the years to come. Once you have established your right to lead, begin to let go systematically, year by year.

5. Don't panic, even during the storms of adolescence. Better times are ahead. A radical turnaround usually occurs in the early twenties.

6. Stay on your child's team, even when it appears to be a losing team. You'll have the rest of your life to enjoy mutual fellowship if you don't overreact to frustration now.

7. Give him time to find himself, even if he appears not to be searching.

8. Most importantly, I urge you to hold your children before the Lord in fervent prayer throughout their years at home. I am convinced that there is no other source of confidence and wisdom in parenting. There is not enough knowledge in the books, mine or anyone else's, to counteract the evil that surrounds our kids today. Our teenagers are confronted by drugs, alcohol, sex, and foul language wherever they turn. And, of course, the peer pressure on them is enormous. We must bathe them in prayer every day of their lives. The God who made your children *will* hear your petitions. He has promised to do so. After all, He loves them more than you do.

Finally, I have a word of encouragement prepared especially for those of you who are depressed today. It is a message written by a loving mother named Joan Mills, who must be a very special lady. She expressed her feelings about her children in an article that initially appeared in a 1981 issue of *Reader's Digest.* It is called "Season of the Empty Nest," and I believe you will be touched by the warmth of these words.

> Remember when the children built blanket tents to sleep in? And then scrambled by moonlight to their own beds, where they'd be safe from bears? And how proud and eager they were to be starting kindergarten? But only up to the minute they got there? And the time they packed cardboard suitcases in such a huff? "You won't see us again!" they hollered. Then they turned back at the end of the yard because they'd forgotten to go to the bathroom.

It's the same thing when they're 20 or 22, starting to make their own way in the grownup world. Bravado, pangs, false starts, and pratfalls. They're half in, half out. "Good-bye, good-bye! Don't worry, Mom!" They're back the first weekend to borrow the paint roller and a fuse and a broom. Prowling the attic, they seize the quilt the dog ate and the terrible old sofa cushions that smell like dead mice. "Just what I need!" they cheer, loading the car.

"Good-bye, good-bye!" implying forever. But they show up without notice at suppertimes, sighing soulfully to see the familiar laden plates. They go away again, further secured by four bags of groceries, the electric frying pan, and a cookbook.

They call home collect, but not as often as parents need to hear. And their news makes fast-graying hair stand on end: ". . . so he forgot to set the brake, and he says my car rolled three blocks backward down the hill before it was totaled!" ". . . simple case of last hired, first fired, no big deal. I sold the stereo, and . . ."

"Mom! Everybody in the city has them! There's this roach stuff you put under the sink. It's . . ."

I gripped the phone with both hands in those days, wishing I could bribe my children back with everything they'd ever wanted—drum lessons, a junk-food charge account, anything. I struggled with an unbecoming urge to tell them once more about hot breakfasts and crossing streets and dry socks on wet days.

"I'm so impressed by how you cope!" I said instead.

The children scatter, and parents draw together, remembering sweetshaped infants heavy in their arms,

233

patched jeans, chicken pox, the night the accident happened, the rituals of Christmases and proms. With wistful pride and a feeling for the comic, they watch over their progeny from an effortfully kept distance. It is the season of the empty nest.

Slowly, slowly, there are changes. Something wonderful seems to hover then, faintly heard, glimpsed in illumined moments. Visiting the children, the parents are almost sure of it.

A son spreads a towel on the table and efficiently irons a perfect crease into his best pants. (*Ironing boards*, his mother thinks, adding to a mental shopping list.) "I'm taking you to a French restaurant for dinner," the young man announces. "I've made reservations."

"Am I properly dressed?" his mother asks, suddenly shy. He walks her through city streets within the aura of his assurance. His arm lies lightly around her shoulders.

Or a daughter offers her honored guest the only two chairs she has and settles into a harem heap of floor pillows. She has raised plants from cuttings, framed a wall full of prints herself, spent three weekends refinishing the little dresser that glows in a square of sun.

Her parents regard her with astonished love. The room has been enchanted by her touch. "Everything's charming," they tell her honestly. "It's a real home.

"Now? Is it *now?* Yes. The something wonderful descends. The generations smile at one another, as if exchanging congratulations. The children are no longer children. The parents are awed to discover adults.

It *is* wonderful, in ways my imagination had not begun to dream on. How could I have guessed—how could they?—that of my three, the shy one would pluck a dazzling array of competencies out of the air and turn up, chatting with total poise, on TV shows? That the one who turned his adolescence into World War III would find his role in arduous, sensitive human service? Or that the unbookish, antic one, torment of his teachers, would evolve into a scholar, tolerating a student's poverty and writing into the night?

I hadn't suspected that my own young adults would be so ebulliently funny one minute, and so tellingly introspective the next: so openhearted and unguarded. Or that growing up would inspire them to buy life insurance and three-piece suits and lend money to the siblings they'd once robbed of lollipops. Or that walking into their houses, I'd hear Mozart on the tape player and find books laid out for me to borrow.

Once, long ago, I waited nine months at a time to see who they would be, babes newly formed and wondrous. "Oh, *look!* I said, and fell in love. Now my children are wondrously new to me in a different way. I am in love again.

My daughter and I freely share the complex world of our inner selves, and all the other worlds we know. Touched, I notice how her rhythms and gestures are reminding of her grandmother's or mine. We are linked by unconscious mysteries and benignly watched by ghosts. I turn my head to gaze at her. She meets my look and smiles.

A son flies the width of the country for his one vacation in a whole long year. He follows me around the kitchen, tasting from the pots, handing down the dishes.

We brown in the sun. Read books in silent synchrony.

PARENTING ISN'T FOR COWARDS

He jogs. I tend the flowers. We walk at the unfurled edge of great waves. We talk and talk, and later play cribbage past midnight. I'm utterly happy.

"But it's your vacation!" I remind him. "What shall we do that's special?"

"This," he says. "Exactly this."

When my children first ventured out and away, I felt they were in flight to outer space, following a curve of light and time to such unknowns that my heart would surely go faint with trying to follow. I thought this would be the end of parenting. Not what it is—the best part; the final, firmest bonding; the goal and the reward.[1]

Appendix

Questionnaire for Parents about Their Children Whom They Believe to Be Strong-Willed or Compliant

I. The items in this section ask general questions about you as a parent.

A. Individual completing this survey:

Mother ☐   Father ☐   Both parents together ☐

B. Mother (if you are the father answering for the mother, please circle the number you think she would have circled).
As a child, I was:

Very Strong-Willed	Strong-Willed	Neither	Very Compliant	Compliant
1	2	3	4	5

C. Father (if you are the mother answering for the father, please circle the number you think he would have circled):
As a child, I was:

Very Strong-Willed	Strong-Willed	Neither	Very Compliant	Compliant
1	2	3	4	5

237

PARENTING ISN'T FOR COWARDS

II. Even though this questionnaire deals only with your oldest strong-willed or compliant child (if any), it is important to know how you evaluate the temperament of all your children. Please rate them on the scale below.

	First-Born	Second-Born	Third-Born	Fourth-Born	Fifth-Born	Sixth-Born	Seventh-Born
Sex M/F	—	—	—	—	—	—	—
Current Age	—	—	—	—	—	—	—

Please circle one characteristic below:

Children	Very Compliant	Cooper-ative	Average	Uncooper-ative	Very Strong-Willed
Firstborn	1	2	3	4	5
Secondborn	1	2	3	4	5
Thirdborn	1	2	3	4	5
Fourthborn	1	2	3	4	5
Fifthborn	1	2	3	4	5
Sixthborn	1	2	3	4	5
Seventhborn	1	2	3	4	5

III. The items in this section ask questions about your child(ren) whom you consider to be either strong-willed or compliant. It is possible that you had more than one child in each category. If so, please answer the questions for the oldest strong-willed child and/or the oldest compliant child. If you only had a child in one of the two categories, please ignore the other. If you had children who were neither strong-willed nor compliant, please place an "X"_____ here and return the questionnaire to us uncompleted.

	Strong-Willed Child	Compliant Child
A. Sex:	M ☐ F ☐	M ☐ F ☐
B. Current age:	_____	_____
C. Order of birth (lst, 2nd, . . .):	_____	_____

D. Age at which the temperament was first recognized:

	Strong-Willed Child M ☐ F ☐	Compliant Child M ☐ F ☐
Birth to 3 months:	_____	_____
3 to 6 months:	_____	_____
6 to 12 months:	_____	_____
1 to 3 years:	_____	_____
3 to 6 years:	_____	_____

E. Discipline of father (if you are the mother answering for the father, circle the number you think he would have circled):

Strong-Willed Child

Permissive 1	Rather Easy 2	Average 3	Rather Strict 4	Rigid and severe 5

Compliant Child

Permissive 1	Rather Easy 2	Average 3	Rather Strict 4	Rigid and severe 5

F. Discipline of mother (if you are the father answering for the mother, circle the number you think she would have circled):

Strong-Willed Child

Permissive 1	Rather Easy 2	Average 3	Rather Strict 4	Rigid and severe 5

Compliant Child

Permissive 1	Rather Easy 2	Average 3	Rather Strict 4	Rigid and severe 5

PARENTING ISN'T FOR COWARDS

G. The amount of stress created for the parents by the child's temperament: (Note: "1" indicates that the child was a joy to raise and caused virtually no disharmony or agitation for the parents; "2" means the child was generally pleasant and easy to raise; "3" means average, "4" means the child was generally difficult to raise; "5" means the child was unpleasant and caused great disharmony and agitation in the home.)

Strong-Willed Child

Total Joy	Generally Pleasant	Average	Difficult	Unpleasant
1	2	3	4	5

Compliant Child

Total Joy	Generally Pleasant	Average	Difficult	Unpleasant
1	2	3	4	5

H. Which parent related to and handled the child best at each age level?

Strong-Willed Child

Age	Mother	Father	Only One Parent Present	Neither Parent Did Well
0–2	1	2	3	4
2–4	1	2	3	4
4–6	1	2	3	4
6–13	1	2	3	4
13–20	1	2	3	4
20 to present	1	2	3	4

Compliant Child

Age	Mother	Father	Only One Parent Present	Neither Parent Did Well
0–2	1	2	3	4
2–4	1	2	3	4
4–6	1	2	3	4
6–13	1	2	3	4
13–20	1	2	3	4
20 to present	1	2	3	4

I. Degree of rebellion against adult authority and values at each age level:

Strong-Willed Child

Age	Complete Acceptance	Rather Cooperative	Average Response	Rather-Deficient	Total Rejection
0–2	1	2	3	4	5
2–4	1	2	3	4	5
4–6	1	2	3	4	5
6–13	1	2	3	4	5
13–20	1	2	3	4	5
20 to present	1	2	3	4	5

Compliant Child

Age	Complete Acceptance	Rather Cooperative	Average Response	Rather-Deficient	Total Rejection
0–2	1	2	3	4	5
2–4	1	2	3	4	5
4–6	1	2	3	4	5
6–13	1	2	3	4	5
13–20	1	2	3	4	5
20 to present	1	2	3	4	5

PARENTING ISN'T FOR COWARDS

J. Describe the temperament of your child at *each* age level up to the present time (or to age 24, if applicable):

Strong-Willed Child

Age	Very Compliant	Cooperative	Average	Very Uncooperative	Defiant
1–2	1	2	3	4	5
3–4	1	2	3	4	5
5–6	1	2	3	4	5
7–8	1	2	3	4	5
9–10	1	2	3	4	5
11–12	1	2	3	4	5
13–14	1	2	3	4	5
15–16	1	2	3	4	5
17–18	1	2	3	4	5
19–20	1	2	3	4	5
21–22	1	2	3	4	5
23–24	1	2	3	4	5

Compliant Child

Age	Very Compliant	Cooperative	Average	Very Uncooperative	Defiant
1–2	1	2	3	4	5
3–4	1	2	3	4	5
5–6	1	2	3	4	5
7–8	1	2	3	4	5
9–10	1	2	3	4	5
11–12	1	2	3	4	5
13–14	1	2	3	4	5
15–16	1	2	3	4	5
17–18	1	2	3	4	5
19–20	1	2	3	4	5
21–22	1	2	3	4	5
23–24	1	2	3	4	5

K. Has your grown child (age 20 or older) accepted your values and established a good working relationship with you as his parents?

Strong-Willed Child

Yes	No	Somewhat	N/A
1	2	3	4

Compliant Child

Yes	No	Somewhat	N/A
1	2	3	4

L. Social adjustment at each age level:

Strong-Willed Child

Age	No Social Problems	Generally Liked	Average Response	Generally Disliked	Many Social Problems
4–6	1	2	3	4	5
6–13	1	2	3	4	5
13–20	1	2	3	4	5
20 to present	1	2	3	4	5

Compliant Child

Age	No Social Problems	Generally Liked	Average Response	Generally Disliked	Many Social Problems
4–6	1	2	3	4	5
6–13	1	2	3	4	5
13–20	1	2	3	4	5
20 to present	1	2	3	4	5

M. Influence of friends at each age level:

Strong-Willed Child

Age	No Influence by Peers	Little Influence by Peers	Average Response	Major Influence by Peers	Extremely Vulnerable to Peers
4–6	1	2	3	4	5
6–13	1	2	3	4	5
13–20	1	2	3	4	5
20 to present	1	2	3	4	5

Compliant Child

Age	No Influence by Peers	Little Influence by Peers	Average Response	Major Influence by Peers	Extremely Vulnerable to Peers
4–6	1	2	3	4	5
6–13	1	2	3	4	5
13–20	1	2	3	4	5
20 to present	1	2	3	4	5

N. Self-Concept:

Strong-Willed Child

Age	Excellent Self-Image	Generally Accepted Himself	Average Response	Generally Disliked Himself	Extreme Self-Hatred
4–6	1	2	3	4	5
6–13	1	2	3	4	5
13–20	1	2	3	4	5
20 to present	1	2	3	4	5

Compliant Child

Age	Excellent Self-Image	Generally Accepted Himself	Average Response	Generally Disliked Himself	Extreme Self-Hatred
4–6	1	2	3	4	5
6–13	1	2	3	4	5
13–20	1	2	3	4	5
20 to present	1	2	3	4	5

O. School achievement, generally, at each age level:
(Note: Scale the same as common grading scale in school: "A" outstanding; "C" average; "F" fail.)

	Strong-Willed Child	**Compliant Child**
Preschool	A B C D F	A B C D F
Grades 1–6	A B C D F	A B C D F
Grades 7–9	A B C D F	A B C D F
Grades 10–12	A B C D F	A B C D F
College	A B C D F	A B C D F
Post College	A B C D F	A B C D F

P. For your child who is now grown, how well has he or she achieved in life?

Strong-Willed Child

Highly Successful 1	Rather Successful 2	Average 3	Rather Unsuccessful 4	Very Unsuccessful 5

Compliant Child

Highly Successful 1	Rather Successful 2	Average 3	Rather Unsuccessful 4	Very Unsuccessful 5

Q. Speaking generally, circle the number of the sentence that best describes how you feel about raising your strong-willed child:

1. It has been a struggle that has often left me depressed, guilt-ridden, and exhausted.
2. It has been difficult but exciting and rewarding too.
3. It has been a very positive experience.
4. He/she was difficult in the early years, but the adolescent years were less stormy and difficult.

PARENTING ISN'T FOR COWARDS

R. Speaking generally, select the sentence that best describes how you feel about raising your compliant child:

1. It has been a struggle that has often left me depressed, guilt-ridden, and exhausted.
2. It has been difficult but exciting and rewarding too.
3. It has been a very positive experience.
4. He/she was a joy in the early years, but adolescence was extremely stressful for both generations.

Thank you so much for your help in conducting this informal research project.

Study Guide

❦

Parenting Isn't for Cowards

Discussion Questions

Chapter 1–The Challenge

1. Review the next-to-last paragraph on page 2 about the confident woman unaware her slip had collapsed. What, concerning parenting, has been *your* "collapsed slip"—what has surprised you about your job as a parent that seems more challenging than you would have thought?

2. Describe an embarrassing moment you have had with your child, similar to that on page 3 of the mom who took her toddler to the Muppet movie.

3. Look at the list on page 4, quoting parents who feel inadequate. Have any situations with your child during the last year caused you to feel inadequate? Identify the quotes with which you can relate.

4. From pages 6–9, what are some of the challenges of our time for parents—challenges unique to this era in our culture?

5. What are some things Dr. Dobson says on page 9 will be discussed in the following chapters, and which topics interest you the most?

Chapter 2–The Tough and the Gentle

1. After reading page 11, tell what *you* might be found muttering on one of *your* lying-flat-on-the-floor days.
2. According to page 12, what are some characteristics of children between eighteen and thirty-six months of age?
3. Describe how a tough-minded, or strong-willed, child differs from a more gentle, compliant child. (See pages 13–16 and 20–21.)
4. What were some of the findings of psychiatrists Chess and Thomas (pages 19–20) regarding how babies differ? Into what three categories did most of the children they studied fit?
5. Generally speaking, is your child one of the *tough* or the *gentle?*

Chapter 3–What 35,000 Parents Said About Their Children

Note to Leader: This topic will take two sessions to cover well. Also, the following agenda works best if the group has *not* read this particular chapter beforehand.

1. On a separate sheet of paper, list your answers to the test on pages 23–27. (Leader, hand out paper and pencils. Read questions aloud as the parents take the test.)
2. Score your test as we look together at the answers given on pages 28–38. If you answered correctly,

tell the group how you knew the answer. If your answer differed from the poll results, discuss how knowing the *norm* now might help you in parenting.

3. How can seeing up the road—knowing the *tendencies* of your child based on his or her personality—help you to "steer around" pitfalls you might otherwise drive straight into?

4. What did you learn about strong-willed children . . .
   a. that most encourages you?
   b. that most prepares you for the challenge?

5. What new things did you learn about the easygoing child? What are some steps you can take to give that child the attention needed but not usually demanded?

6. How does Table 5 on page 41 relate to King Solomon's proverb about children generally following their parents' values by the time they are older? (See Proverbs 22:6. Chapter 10, "Questions and Answers," on pages 183–210 gives further insight on this.)

Chapter 4–What 35,000 Parents Said About Themselves

1. At what did one-third of those parents who were polled feel like failures? (See page 45.) Would you guess that their children were compliant or strong-willed?

2. According to page 46, how did 95 percent of the parents of compliant children feel about the job they were doing in parenting? What percentage of the parents of strong-willed children felt they were doing a good job as parents? Now cite the percentages that show which parents were struggling the most.

3. Can you control whether your child is compliant or strong-willed by nature? Do you think parents' frustration levels might be lessened if they didn't see their children's personalities and temperaments as reflections of their parenting styles?
4. How does the poll reveal that mothers, especially, react to strong-willed children? (See pages 48–52.)
5. How does the frustration that parents of strong-willed children feel affect the way they discipline? (See pages 58–59.) What does this teach us about loving, *consistent* discipline?

Chapter 5–With Love to Parents Who Hurt

1. Do you suspect that you have known fairly well, at some point in your life, a "low-flying kid" (as described on page 56), either in your family, circle of friends, or perhaps one of your own children? To what was the child's difference due—physical handicap, learning disability, peculiar personality, or something else? Have you ever seen an initially-low-flying kid eventually soar in some area? If so, please describe what happened.
2. Read an encouraging story in 1 Samuel 16:1, 6–13, where God picked an unlikely young shepherd boy as king, rather than one of his brothers who seemed more fit. How does this story about David encourage you? Why do you think God likes to choose *unlikely* people to do great things?
3. Referring to the two stories on pages 59–61 about the two very different toddlers, how do you think their moms felt during those plane rides?

4. Refer to the letter on pages 66–68 and Dr. Dobson's comments about it on pages 68–69. Then turn back to pages 41–42. How would knowing these facts comfort the mother who wrote the letter on pages 66–68? What Scripture backs up the finding that most of the difficult kids eventually do stabilize and return to parental values? (See Proverbs 22:6 again.)

5. What part does prayer have in good parenting? (See pages 71–74.) How did Dr. and Mrs. Dobson pray for their children in their developmental years? (See page 72.)

6. Who modeled a good prayer life for Dr. Dobson, and how did that person's prayers affect Dr. Dobson's father at a pivotal point in his life? (See pages 72–74.)

7. Who has modeled for all of us the importance of loving and praying for children? (See Matthew 19:13–15 and Mark 10:13–16.)

Chapter 6–Suggestions for Parents of Young Children, Part 1

1. While many parents feel false guilt over circumstances beyond their control, for what exactly *should* parents be feeling responsibility regarding their children? (See page 75, and Matthew 18:5–6, 10.)

2. What does Susan's story on page 79 illustrate? What was Jesus' answer to people who turned children away from Him? (See Mark 10:13–16.)

3. Look for some ways that Dr. Dobson suggests parents can *go with the flow* of their child's particular make-ups and express acceptance . . .

PARENTING ISN'T FOR COWARDS

a. from page 80, second paragraph.

b. from page 80, third paragraph through page 81, third paragraph.

c. from page 81, fourth paragraph through page 82, fifth paragraph.

4. Refer to the description on pages 82–83 of the mom who felt *unable* to take the temperature of her six-month-old because he wouldn't let her. Describe your own *thermometer experience* of late—a recent situation in which you and your child met head-on over something needful. Tell how you handled it or determined to handle it next time.

5. What did Susannah Wesley, an effective eighteenth-century mom of *seventeen* children, write about how and why she grabbed the reins of authority early? (See pages 83–84.)

6. What is the difference between "childish follies" and "willful transgressions"? (See page 85.)

7. What is appropriate loving firmness? (See pages 86–87.) What is the parallel between a young child's ability to easily learn languages, and his teachableness in other areas during his early years? (See page 88.)

8. What is "sibling drift," and how can parents maintain a consistency with each new child's arrival? (See pages 88–89.)

Chapter 6–Suggestions for Parents of Young Children, Part 2

1. Describe the three pitfalls that parents of very compliant children must avoid. (See pages 91–92.)

2. Read Luke 15:11–32 (also refer to pages 92–94) and describe . . .

252

a. the strong-willed son's actions.

b. why the compliant son reacted so bitterly when his brother was royally welcomed home.

3. Why and how do compliant children sometimes embark on quests for control in non-confrontal but dangerous ways? (See pages 94–95.)

4. What are six things parents can do to prevent or deal with these types of challenges with compliant kids? (See pages 95–96.)

5. Recall the letter on pages 96–97 from the mother of the "rolled baby." Relate an incident that had *you* "rolling in the aisle" in laughter over your kid's antics. Proverbs 17:22 (NCV) says, "A happy heart is like good medicine." If laughter is sometimes the best medicine for weary parents, what situations most often help you to take regular doses?

6. What instruction does the Bible give to parents in Ephesians 6:4 and Deuteronomy 6:4–9? (Also see pages 100–101.) When does Deuteronomy tell us to talk about God with our children?

7. Why do you think it's important to weave talk of God into the fabric of our children's daily lives? How are you doing that?

8. What experiences deeply influenced Dr. Dobson's faith as a child and young person? (See pages 100–103.)

Chapter 7—Power Games

1. For what do strong-willed children thirst more than compliant ones? (See pages 105–106.)

2. Review the list of sixteen techniques on pages 107–108 that are often used in power struggles,

especially in families. Which of these manipulations have you observed in *power games* played by members of your family?

3. Over what issues do children often assert themselves? (See headings on pages 109–113.) At what ages of childhood do these issues normally become battlefields:

a. bedtime?

b. food?

c. schoolwork?

4. What is it about special days that tends to bring on battles? (See pages 113–116.)

5. What are some other battlefields of childhood listed on page 116?

6. Over what issues does your child seem to regularly wage war?

7. Give some historical examples of the destructive results of power. (See pages 117–120.)

8 What did Jesus tell His disciples when they argued over which of them would have the highest positions of power in His coming kingdom? (Read Matthew 20:20–28.)

9. What is our goal as parents regarding the transfer of power to our children? (See page 122.)

Chapter 8–Too Pooped to Parent

1. Which parents are the most likely candidates for parental burnout? (See pages 123–124.)

2. Describe a compulsive parent. (See pages 124–126.) What factors contribute to compulsive parenting? What relationships tend to suffer because of it?

3. Are the underlying motives of *superparents* basically admirable? (See page 126.) List the five main insights on how burnout occurs. (See page 127.)

4. What example concerning balance did Jesus give? (See page 128.) Why do you think God rested for a day after He had created the world? (See Genesis 2:2–3.) Was He modeling something for us?

5. What factors, other than deep commitment to parenting, can lead to burnout?

6. Describe the five progressive stages of burnout. (See pages 128–136.) Have you experienced any of these?

7. What are the three *departments* of our beings? (See pages 135–136.) How does one affect the other?

8. How is raising children like running a long-distance race? (See page 136.)

9. To prevent parenting burnout, how are you taking care of your . . .
   a. body?
   b. mind?
   c. spirit?

Chapter 9–Suggestions for Parents of Adolescents, Part 1

1. How is adolescence like the liftoff, reentry, and splashdown of a spacecraft? (See pages 137–138.)

2. What two powerful forces overtake boys and girls in early adolescence? (See pages 139–146.)

3. How is adolescence similar to PMS, menopause, or mid-life crisis? (See pages 140–141.)

4. How does acceptance or rejection from an adolescent's peers influence self-worth and behavior? (See pages 141–146.)

5. List the five vital areas Dr. Dobson will be discussing for parents of teenagers. (See headings on pages 147–181.) Which of the headings hint at an answer to something about which you are curious?

6. What were *your* teen years like? What made them . . .
   a. harder?
   b. easier?

7. What would you do differently from your parents as you parent a teen? What will you try to do the same as they did?

8. Why is boredom dangerous for teens? (See page 147.) List some activities parents can encourage in order to prevent boredom in their teenagers.

9. When can parents expect teen turbulence to peak and then level off again? (See pages 147–148.)

Chapter 9–Suggestions for Parents of Adolescents, Part 2

1. What does Dr. Dobson mean when he says . . .
   a. "Don't throw away your friendship over behavior that has no great moral significance"? (See page 150.)
   b. "Save your big guns for crucial confrontations"? (Page 150)

  c. "The philosophy we applied with our teenagers can be called 'loosen and tighten'"? (Pages 151–152)

2. Should parents ever apologize when they are wrong? (See pages 152–153.)

3. What four suggestions will help keep you from burnout while parenting an adolescent? (See page 155.)

4. Dr. Dobson said about his feelings as a teen, "How could I get angry at this man who took time to be with me?" Of what man was he speaking? (See pages 158–159.)

5. What does Ephesians 6:4 tell fathers to be careful *not* to do?

6. What common-ground interests are being cultivated between your children and their dad, or a father-image in their lives, and why is that vital? (See pages 156–165.)

7. If you are a mom, how have you *interpreted* your children's father to them? (See pages 160–161.)

8. What are some ways a father uniquely influences his daughter, either positively or negatively? (See pages 161–163.)

9. What can be a result of parents letting their teens be *in charge?* (See pages 165–167.)

10. What can be done when parental leadership has collapsed, and a teen continually breaks the law, intimidates his family, and refuses boundaries? (See pages 167–181.) Describe the TOUGHLOVE concept.

Chapter 10—Questions and Answers

Option 1: "I Think Dr. Dobson Would Say . . .

Play the game "I Think Dr. Dobson Would Say. . .". The group leader should read the first question on page 183 aloud, asking the group to keep their books closed while various class members suggest possible answers. Then the group may turn to the appropriate page and see how close they came to answering in a way similar to Dr. Dobson's answer.

Emphasize that everyone's opinion within the group, based on their own parenting experiences, may give added insight. But hold up the Bible as the ultimate authority.

Continue in this manner, throughout the questions and answers in this chapter.

Option 2: Small Group Discussions

Divide the group into four smaller groups, and assign each group three questions. (The group who draws the question with the shortest answer on page 204 should get an extra question. That group should divide the thirteen questions fairly among the four groups.)

Give the small groups about ten to fifteen minutes to read their assigned questions and answers and to prepare to give the whole group a summary of the answers.

Then regather the groups into one large group, and let each of the four groups take turns reading one of their questions aloud and summarizing Dr. Dobson's answer. Continue through all the questions. To make it more fun, place a chair in the front labeled "Dr.

Dobson's Chair," and let each person *answering for* Dr. Dobson come and sit there when speaking.

Chapter 11–Releasing Your Grown Child

1. What was the question asked of Focus on the Family radio listeners, which prompted replies that show the need for this chapter? (See page 211.)
2. What did 44 percent of the 2,600 respondents to the question say? (See page 212.)
3. How did Dr. Dobson himself struggle with these issues at times, both . . .
   a. as a young adult striving for independence from parents? (See pages 213–214.)
   b. as a parent struggling to grant independence to his own children? (See pages 215–216.)
4. Why do you think it's so hard for parents to let go? (See pages 215–216.)
5. What are two common responses of young adults whose parents won't let go? (See pages 216–218.)
6. Why do adult children sometimes refuse to become independent? (See pages 220–222.)
7. Describe a good *transfer-of-power* plan which, if put into play from the time children are in preschool, might help parents be ready to let go by the end of the teen years. (See pages 222–223.)

Chapter 12–A Final Thought

1. What would you say to answer the question of the puzzled mother on page 225?

PARENTING ISN'T FOR COWARDS

2. What three examples does Dr. Dobson give on pages 226–230 of how kids can be totally surprising?

3. Why does Dr. Dobson feel that behavioral scientists have been far too simplistic in their explanation of human behavior? (See page 228.) In that regard, explain how you interpret this quote from page 228: "The same boiling water that softens the carrot also hardens the egg."

4. In an earlier survey of 3,000 parents, what did 85 percent of the families have in common?

5. Read the list of eight final thoughts on pages 231–232, which summarize this book's concepts. (Consider letting the group members take turns reading them aloud.) Out of these thoughts that have been expressed, which ones . . .

   a. were new concepts to you?
   b. answered questions you'd been puzzling over.
   c. gave you specific plans for dealing with certain aspects of parenting?
   d. underlined what you've already experienced?
   e. helped you to more fully understand and accept your children?
   f. encouraged you?
   g. pointed you to your Source, the Creator?